Dispatches from
the Global Village

Dispatches from the Global Village

Derek Evans

CopperHouse

Editor: Mike Schwartzentruber
Cover and interior design: Verena Velten
Proofreader: Merlin Beltain
Cover photos: © Stafan Klein/iStockphoto *(photo album)*
        All other photos used by permission. Source: *(clockwise from the*
        top left) Amnesty International, Palestine Authority, Amnesty
        International, Derek Evans, Amnesty International, Derek Evans

WoodLake is an imprint of Wood Lake Publishing, Inc. Wood Lake Publishing
acknowledges the financial support of the Government of Canada, through
the Book Publishing Industry Development Program (BPIDP) for its publishing
activities. Wood Lake Publishing also acknowledges the financial support of the
Province of British Columbia through the Book Publishing Tax Credit.

 **BRONZE**

BNC CERTIFIED | BIBLIOGRAPHIC DATA 2006-07

At Wood Lake Publishing, we practise what we publish, being guided by a
concern for fairness, justice, and equal opportunity in all of our relationships
with employees and customers. Wood Lake Publishing is an employee-owned
company, committed to caring for the environment and all creation. Wood Lake
Publishing recycles, reuses, and encourages readers to do the same. Resources
are printed on 100% post-consumer recycled paper and more environmentally
friendly groundwood papers (newsprint), whenever possible. A percentage of all
profit is donated to charitable organizations.

Library and Archives Canada Cataloguing in Publication

A catalogue record for this publication is available from the
National Library of Canada.

ISBN 978-1-551455-53-2

Published by WoodLake
An imprint of Wood Lake Publishing Inc.
9590 Jim Bailey Road, Kelowna, BC, Canada, V4V 1R2
www.woodlakebooks.com
250.766.2778

Printing 10 9 8 7 6 5 4 3 2 1
Printed in Canada by Houghton Boston, Saskatoon, SK

 100%
ANCIENT FOREST post-consumer
FRIENDLY recycled paper

For Pat,
my sense of home, my source of direction,
my companion on so many journeys,
and ever my destination.

Contents

Foreword

Derek Evans is a gentle soul with a will of iron. As a friend and as a leader, as a mediator and as a guide, he is open and honest, disarming and kind. And yet hidden within that deep serenity is a burning essence of universal curiosity – a conflagration that rages but is never consumed, a phenomenon of creative agitation, unknown, at times, even to himself.

Perhaps it is just this dual disposition that makes him so uniquely successful. Derek is both artist and scientist; he trusts his intuition and will leap into the heart of the deepest abyss, but, at the same time, he engages in excruciating research before operating in some of the most sensitive theatres of unfolding world history.

While this contemplative, anecdotal volume touches heaven and embraces the earth, it is always centred in the heart of hope. Evans' interests – as evidenced by the one-word titles in this lithe book – are multidisciplinary maps of the universe. He speaks of politics with the maturity of an elder statesman, yet his decades of political activism have not discouraged him from appreciating the highest potential of human goodness. Evans takes us sailing through improbable deserts, and buffeting into human storms more terrible than nature ever conceived. We join him on the battlefield and at the negotiating table; we are drawn to tears of blood by the tragic death of individuals, tribes and towns, who all, in their innocence, were devoured by the crazed ambassadors of Darkness. We know now what it is like to feel unrelenting despair, as Evans describes the kidnapping and the torture of too many victims and unwilling martyrs, and brings us face to face with the war-worn faces of child soldiers, barely ten years old.

In the midst of this global horror, Evans introduces us to a diplomacy of light. He shares his healing dreams by walking us along the peace of a faraway lake, and by inviting us to stroll in his gardens – be they on rooftops or terraces, in old swimming pools, city plots, or backyard acreages. He guides us through passages in his memory, where we join him in distant jungles, mountain strongholds, and urban oases. Bells ring, awakening the air; and fragrant foods – when drought is not master – are served throughout this peripatetic tour of one man's unique life.

Derek Evans is a kind of Forrest Gump or even TinTin character: you get the feeling that he has been everywhere, met everyone, and done everything... and that even if he hasn't, he soon will. He has met prime ministers and presidents, rebels and kings, beggars and saints, terrorists and scholars, generals and chiefs. His travels have propelled him through dozens of countries on almost every continent on earth. These essays, thankfully, bring him home to us where, for a moment, we can begin to appreciate this magnificent man in our midst.

Yosef Wosk, Ph.D., OBC

Director of Interdisciplinary Programs, Simon Fraser University;
and Founder of the Canadian Academy of Independent Scholars,
and of the Philosophers' Café, Vancouver

Introduction

Naramata is an extraordinarily beautiful village nestled on the shores of Okanagan Lake in southern British Columbia. The tourist brochures portray its vineyards and villas as a tiny pocket of Tuscany hidden amid the forests and mountains of the Pacific northwest, and the single road that reaches out to the village comes to an end at a place called Paradise Ranch. The village consists of fewer than a thousand households, and the word "idyllic" is often heard slipping from the conversations of visitors strolling along a country lane. You get the picture.

I had the privilege of calling Naramata "home" for about six years, after returning to Canada from a decade based in London – a place with rather more people but somewhat less prodigious natural beauty. It made for quite a transition! I soon discovered that the most significant difference between the two places had nothing to do with either their size, or with the external environment. It had to do with the particular quality of neighbourliness that characterized the village.

The village is proud of being an "unincorporated" community, but this lack of formal structure and organization seemed to engender a greater and more active level of genuine dialogue and democratic debate than I had ever experienced elsewhere. Soon after arriving, the people who published the village's periodic newspaper asked me to contribute a regular column, something on "the world, ideas, and stuff." Given my own temperament, I couldn't imagine a more appropriate beat for me to try to "cover." Once a month, I dutifully sat down to fulfill the unbounded range of my mandate.

What never failed to astonish me was not only that my neighbours actually read these columns, but the extent to which they did so. It seemed that everyone in the village read my monthly musings – indeed, they read them with some care and even debated them around their kitchen tables or over morning coffee at the Village Grounds café. A visit to the farmers' market or to the pub inevitably involved several discussions with neighbours on precise issues of detail they had noted to raise with me – often related to something I'd written two or three months previously, and had completely forgotten.

Before long, I had a keen sense of the ultimate of journalistic joys – of being involved in an extended conversation with my neighbours, and even of being accompanied by my community as my work took me to difficult situations in different parts of the world. I began to refer to these columns as my Naramata "sutras" – a term which usually refers to a short Buddhist text, but which actually means "thread." It draws from the same ancient Sanskrit root word from which we get "suture," the thread we use to bind wounds.

While the topics or occasions of these pieces may vary widely (such is my life!), the notion of a sutra or thread seems to reflect well the theme and character that holds these pieces together. On the one hand, they seek to combine the experience of personal memoir with an engagement of the present moment. On the other hand, they are an effort to form a perspective, to articulate a worldview that explores and is informed by an appreciation of the intimate linkage between the local and global realities of the world. In all cases, they reflect something of my own groping search for the path to peace and justice, that frayed and elusive thread that may guide us through the dark and tangled forest of fear and hatred that continues to tear us apart.

And, of course, these essays have been written as letters home, as expressions of the thread or spirit that binds friends and neighbours together despite time and distance. I hope that as you share in these reflections you too will feel welcomed, and at home with neighbours.

The author's royalties and a portion of the publisher's profits from this book will be donated to two charities: the Naramata Community Fund, which provides emergency assistance to local people in need; and Amnesty International, which provides emergency support to people in need throughout the global village.

1 Walls

We are all connected to each other. I believe that this is a great spiritual truth, perhaps the greatest and the only one we need. I call it a spiritual truth, because I think we really are connected, and yet it seems that so much is done to convince us otherwise. Even though I know it to be true, I am astonished at the way the power of that connection continually eludes me, and am aware that I need constantly to be "converted" to it in the daily reality of my own life.

Sure, there are lots of clichés about globalization, but more often than not they seem to be part of a message intended to reinforce the notion that we are separate or different from others. Too often the messages suggest that we can avoid dealing with the reality of our interdependence through technology or wealth, or they try to convince us that we will be happier if we simply remain ignorant about the needs of others or deny that we care about them.

We go to extraordinary lengths to sustain the myth of separateness. I suppose we do this because the "global village" is, in many ways, a very rough neighbourhood. I grew up in the "space age" of the 1950s and '60s, when astronauts and cosmonauts first soared into orbit and offered humanity a new perspective on this beautiful and fragile planet we share. Yet after half a century, we continue to refer to it conceitedly and possessively as "ours" – as if it were some territory to compete over and carve up – when the glaring truth is that we belong to *it*.

During those decades, it was common for people to say that the Great Wall of China was the only human construction visible from space. In fact, one can see quite a few walls, like scars on the Earth. It seems there is nothing so apparent as the various constructs by which we try to divide the planet and to distinguish ourselves from each other.

You don't need to fly into space to get the message. During the day, at the altitude normally flown by any commercial jet, you can always tell exactly where the border between Mexico and Guatemala lies – it looks as if a razor blade has scored a straight line through the jungle for hundreds of miles. At night, the flood-lights along the fence between India and Pakistan cut a shocking bleached streak across the deserts of south Asia. There are other boundaries that are more noticeable up close, but which are no less impressive – such as the massive concrete trench that separates the two Koreas, or the security barrier or separation fence that is making its inexorable way around Israel and through Palestine. Some of the fences are hardly visible, even up close, such as the line of electronic surveillance cameras gradually encircling the United States. It is ironic that, since the fall of the Berlin Wall in 1989, we are building more and more such structures all over the world; the difference being that we no longer intend them to keep people in, but to keep others out.

Most of our models for dealing with difference, whether personal or political, are built on the delusion that we can avoid conflict, usually through some kind of enforced separation. Even our approach to international peacemaking is often based on an effort to agree to terms of separation, rather than on figuring out how the two sides can live in relation to each other. Even if separation were possible, effective, or desirable, as an approach to conflict and difference it is no longer viable or sustainable. Indeed, it is becoming increasingly dangerous.

The great Okanagan Mountain firestorm will long be remembered in these parts. For decades, the natural cycle of the ponderosa forest was suppressed. This resulted in a buildup of fuel on the forest floor that, once ignited, generated a fire of unprecedented fury, which raged beyond prediction or control. More than 200 homes were destroyed by the firestorm, most of them in areas where human development had recently encroached upon the edge of the wilderness, an area technically known as "the interface zone."

I like that phrase. It emphasizes that the challenge we face is not about building longer walls or wider firebreaks in a futile effort to keep us safe, but about constructing appropriate and respectful relationships with all aspects of the environment in which we live – human and otherwise. Perhaps it is time for us to move away from abstract notions of globalization and to increasingly see ourselves as living in "the interface zone."

2 Killing

Late fall is a powerful time to reflect on the state of our world, and on how to build a healthy and peaceful future. It starts on November 11, Remembrance Day, when we honour all those who have lost their future as a result of war and oppression. It continues to December 10, International Human Rights Day, when we say, "*Nunca más*, never again," and dedicate ourselves to the principle of preventing war and oppression through the promotion and protection of human rights. Christmas, the season dedicated to "peace, and goodwill to all," will soon be upon us, followed by the New Year, when we can resolve to make practical changes for a positive future.

I've recently been doing some research on violence and conflict. During this season, it may be appropriate to reflect on one of my findings. This finding is drawn from what is probably the most extensively studied issue in the social sciences – a problem known as "the major non-participatory trend in warfare." Specifically, studies undertaken throughout the world during the past 150 years – in all wars, on all sides – have demonstrated that, despite appearances, humans possess a powerful and natural resistance to killing other people.[1]

Up to and including World War II, only 15 to 20 percent of soldiers on either side actually fired their weapons with intent to kill – even when faced with a direct personal threat. This finding, though well-documented and consistently proven, was not given a great deal of publicity out of deference to the pride and dignity of veterans. However, military leaders fully recognized the "problem" and following World War II it became the major focus of applied military research, on both sides of the Cold War.

The research determined that there are four main factors that make killing more likely, and that make efforts to encourage killing more efficient. These goals are achieved by:

- ensuring the presence of authority figures on the front lines;
- strengthening the sense of group identity within the military unit;
- fostering emotional distance or a sense of social, moral, and cultural separation from the victim or target;
- increasing the physical distance from the victim or target, ideally to the extent that they no longer exist as a visible, recognizable identity.

These findings led to heavy investment after World War II in technology that would allow troops to engage the enemy without actual contact. As well, emphasis during training focused on strong group identification, and on dehumanization of the enemy – the "boot camp" model of military training we know almost intimately through so many brutal films, such as *Full Metal Jacket*. The proof of the validity of this research and of the effectiveness of these changes came in the pudding. The firing rate in the U.S. forces rose from 20 percent in World War II, to 55 percent in the Korean War, to almost 90 percent in Vietnam.

The research has also consistently shown that only about two percent of individuals in most societies have what is referred to as a "basic predisposition to killing." That is, according to military analysts, fully 98 percent of people are fundamentally disposed *not* to kill other people and must intentionally be trained and equipped to overcome this predisposition. Currently, there is some worrying indication that this basic two percent rate may be rising in our culture, as training in separateness or emotional distancing is increasingly transmitted more generally outside the military, through violence in the media and, in particular, through the predominant characters and themes of computer gaming.

Still, I find in this research a source of real hope. The basic findings suggest that, as a species,

1. We seem to be "hard-wired" *not* to kill;
2. We need to be deliberately taught to overcome this natural tendency, and;
3. We are good learners.

The fact that we are good learners must also mean that we can choose to *unlearn* the myth of our separateness from our "enemies," and can choose to return to and even nurture our "default" or natural resistance to violence and killing. In other words, if we so choose, we can construct a global society based on strategies and practices that build on our natural, God-given connectedness.

---

[1]   See especially Lt. Col. Dave Grossman, *On Killing: The Psychological Cost of Learning to Kill in War and Society* (New York: Little, Brown & Co., 1995).

3 Blanket

One of my most prized possessions is a blanket. It is a beautiful but peculiar thing. Woven from Himalayan yak wool, it stretches more than 20 feet long, and consists of more than 30 separate panels, each with a distinct geometric pattern and an array of earthy colours. I love this blanket because in addition to its intricate patterns and warm colours it also carries a story that is special to me – the story of a man named Tik Nat Rizal.

Tik Nat Rizal was, for many years, an advisor to the King of Bhutan, the small Buddhist country in the Himalayas between India and China. He was also, and continues to be, a man fiercely dedicated to peace, fairness, and justice. He is very determined and stubborn. He is a difficult person.

When a census was carried out in Bhutan in the early 1990s, officials discovered that the Nepali minority would soon constitute half the total population – and were beginning to demand the right to vote. (Most of these Nepalis had entered the country as migrant labourers over the course of the previous decade.) Alarmed, the officials suppressed the census results and elements in the government launched a program designed to force the migrants to leave. Community leaders were imprisoned and abused, a number of villages were attacked and burned, and thousands fled their homes in fear as refugees.

Tik Nat Rizal opposed these repressive actions, and expressed criticism of the government's treatment of the Nepali minority. In an absolute monarchy, the line between criticism of government policy and criticism of the king can be hard to define. Before long, Tik Nat Rizal himself was arrested.

Soldiers went to his house, put him in shackles, and brought him before the king. The king demanded that he retract his views and make an apology. But, as I mentioned, Tik Nat Rizal is a difficult and determined man, a man of principle, and not one to compromise when he believes he is right. He refused to apologize, so the king ordered that he be put in chains and sent to a prison high in the Himalayas, with nothing but the clothes in which he stood.

Tik Nat Rizal likely would have remained there, disappeared and forgotten, perhaps for the rest of his days, huddling in the cold with about a thousand other men who had offended the king, if it hadn't been for one thing – the power of relationship, the fact that we are all deeply connected to each other and can to reach out to each other, and with love can overcome even the greatest barriers.

Before being taken away, Tik Nat Rizal asked for one favour – to be allowed to say goodbye to his wife. Though the king was very angry with him, he also remembered that Tik Nat Rizal was his old friend and had served him well, so he agreed to this request. Tik Nat Rizal's wife was brought to the palace. As Tik Nat Rizal embraced his wife in what both assumed would be their final farewell, he traced a pattern over and over again on her back. The pattern took the following shape: "AI."

Like most people in Bhutan, Tik Nat Rizal's wife was largely illiterate, and certainly had no knowledge of English or of other European languages. At that time there was no radio or television reception in Bhutan, and foreign visitors were limited to 3,000 per year. She had no idea what the mysterious pattern meant, but it was indelibly impressed upon her and she carried it from one friend to another, tracing it on their palms or drawing it on bits of paper. The shape secretly made its way from hand to hand all over the country, until finally, after two years, someone realized its meaning. "I know!" she said. "Those are the Western letters AI." Someone else said, "Ah, he wants you to contact AI – Amnesty International." Tik Nat Rizal himself didn't know anything about Amnesty International, except that it was an organization of people who would help you if you were in trouble.

It took another couple of years for this message to reach Amnesty International headquarters in London, as it travelled from hand to hand, from person to person. But eventually it did so, and arrived on my desk. Diplomatic inquiries were made, and research undertaken with refugees. In the end, the king invited us to meet to discuss a variety of human rights concerns. Though the negotiations were often difficult, after ten days the king agreed to release 963 prisoners, including, last but not least, Tik Nat Rizal.

I'm not sure which person I identify with most in this story. The unyielding man of principle with a hunger for justice, who sometimes becomes a prisoner of his own convictions? Or the proud and powerful man who cannot tolerate criticism and thinks he can deal with problems by locking them away? Or the woman searching for meaning and hope in the face of what seems like mystery and despair at every turn? Or perhaps the friends who tried to help her make sense of it all, and to find a way to act? Or the strangers who offer new perspectives and support for alternate solutions? Maybe the challenge is to try to identify with all of them.

As I was leaving the country, the king presented me with the wonderful yak wool blanket of many different patterns. He said it was a symbol of the ways in which our lives are woven together, even when we don't realize it, even when it sometimes feels as if we live in very distant, very different, very separate worlds.

4 Candles

Among all the thousands of "cases" I worked on during my years with Amnesty International, the one that touched me most deeply occurred in Sri Lanka in the early 1990s. The civil war that had simmered and boiled intermittently for the previous three decades was raging, and terrible atrocities were being committed on all sides.

For most people, every sunset ushered in a time of unbounded fear, and, for some, the deepest horror. The government of the time had declared Amnesty International a "terrorist organization." I was in the country on a low-profile visit, to try to establish a new basis for dialogue with the authorities. One morning, over breakfast with a BBC correspondent, my delegation received a message from one of the most active paramilitary death squads, instructing us to leave the country within 24 hours – a threat and circumstance that immediately made our mission very public and "newsworthy." However, we received other messages during that visit that seemed to touch more deeply the reality of the situation.

Embilipitya is a small town in the south of Sri Lanka, filled with respectable, well-educated, middle-class people of the majority culture. But the civil war had taken hold there as well. Special troops were sent with orders to suppress the insurgency, and the commander met with the local political leaders. Together, they came to a coldly rational conclusion. They instructed the high school teachers to provide lists of the ten best students in each of the senior classes, on the logical assumption that the brightest of the young people would be the ones most likely to criticize the government and to lead the opposition.

Over the next three nights, after darkness fell, the military systematically visited the homes of the 40 young people on the lists and took them away – in many cases, tearing them from the arms of their parents. For a few days, the young people were kept under arrest at a nearby military camp. Their parents could sometimes catch a glimpse of them through a gap in the fence, or when the gate opened for a few moments.

But one night the soldiers broke camp and moved on. The children were nowhere to be found. The parents searched. They made enquiries everywhere, until officials advised that they should stop asking questions, or they and their remaining children might also go missing.

The day after we arrived in the country, a stranger came to see us with a message from the parents of the children who had "disappeared." They asked us to come to their town. I knew that the government and the military were watching my delegation closely, so I sent a message back saying it would not be possible. It would take a day and a night to reach their town from the capital; there were military checkpoints on all the highways; and anyone seen in contact with us would be in great danger. It was a sensible decision, so I put the matter out of my mind, and we went on with our work.

A couple of days later, as I walked down the street, someone slipped a piece of paper into my pocket. The message asked me to come later that night to a church around the corner from my hotel. When it was dark, a colleague and I slipped out for a walk. The church looked shut and empty, but we found the door unlocked, stepped into the silent sanctuary, and closed the door behind us.

After a moment, a match was struck somewhere in the darkness, and a candle was lit, then another and another, until the church seemed full of light. As the light grew, I realized it was also full of people – the parents and grandparents and brothers and sisters of those disappeared young people. The cold and lonely sanctuary became a living, sacred place.

Although they were very afraid, and with good reason, those family members were so full of love for their lost children, and so filled with a hunger for the truth and a determination for justice, that their hearts had no room left for their fear. And although I knew that I was in the presence of a sorrow so deep and a grief so raw that I could not pretend to grasp it, I felt, at the same time, that I had never experienced such overflowing care and love, such compassion and determination. I sensed the very spirit of life, power, and freedom.

The motto of Amnesty International is, "Better to light a candle than to curse the darkness." We worked with those families for the next ten years. Three governments came and went, but the care and commitment of the families, and their dedication to truth and justice, persisted. In the end, we identified the main perpetrators of the abuses, pursued prosecutions against them through the courts, and eventually won convictions for most of those responsible – senior military officers and even the high school principal. We trained a cadre of forensic investigators and exhumed numerous mass graves – work described in Michael Ondaatje's book *Anil's Ghost*. The remains of many children were recovered, but, to this point, not those of the families of Embilipitya.

Why did this case touch me so deeply? I think it is because, though they had much cause, the families seemed never to be motivated by a sense of bitterness or vengeance, but only by their love – for their children, for each other, and for the hope of a healthy future for their country.

Perhaps the most important aspect and challenge of taking responsibility and action in a world of mass terrorism is this determination to keep open not only our minds and hands, but also our hearts.

This is difficult, because it means remaining open, even if it is possible only in some small measure, to sharing the pain of those we seek to understand, of those with whom we seek to be in solidarity. The root of the word *compassion* means to "suffer with." So the discipline of the open heart means that we will inevitably experience hurt, and even a certain scarring during the course of our work and commitment. The great paradox and mystery of our experience, one that often appears at the core of our understanding of spirituality, is that it is precisely in this act of embracing the suffering of another that we may discover a special strength, the possibility of healing, and even grace.

5 Mummies

I find it impossible to walk in the fresh snow on the Kettle Valley trail these early winter mornings and *not* have lines from Robert Frost to mind. *"The woods are lovely, dark and deep..."* Absolutely, beautiful. *"Two roads diverged in a wood, and I took the one less travelled..."* True, wise. *"Good fences make good neighbours."* Well, I'm not so sure.

When I lived in the UK during the 1990s, a study was conducted that found that property disputes consumed more court time than anything else, and that the vast majority of these disputes involved less than six inches. Great Britain is a small island with a large population, so I suppose every bit counts! But I suspect the same dynamic is present in all cultures.

Certainly, all religions place a high priority on rituals of inclusion, such as baptism, which are intended to welcome new members into a community. Unfortunately, too often they also act as symbolic practices of *exclusion*, as ways to express how special "we" are by emphasizing the line separating "us" from "them." Of course, we exercise these divisions not only in our religions, but also in our political and other systems.

A wonderful example from recent archaeology illustrates this dynamic: the story of the red-haired mummies of Xingjiang. The oldest and best-preserved human remains in the world were found in the mid-1990s in the deserts of north-western China. Traditionally, the Chinese government has treated any scientific achievement as triumphant news, proof of the wisdom of the ruling party. But in this case the discovery was seen as a threat and so they attempted to suppress the story. However, as the old saying goes, "Truth will out." Word slowly began to seep out around the edges of the scientific community and finally, in 2001, the Chinese government "released" the "news."

The reason they had tried to conceal the story lies in a carefully constructed sentence on the second page of the Xinghua press statement: "Archaeologists have theorized that the newly found mummies were Indo-European men, judging from the facial structure and size of the bodies." In fact, the mummies are so well preserved that some of them still have their red hair, and their tartan plaid clothing! Some graves contained both Caucasian and Han people buried together. Apparently, they lived together – peaceably and in prosperity![1]

This picture of ancient multicultural harmony did not fit comfortably with the official story of the Chinese state – of a society dominated by the Han majority, of the separate and independant development of the Middle Kingdom.

Most societies, many families, and even many individuals strive to sustain some version of the myth of separateness. Somehow, our sense of being special seems to depend more on our perceived differences from others – notions that too often need to be reinforced with "good fences" – than on what we share together. Indeed, as the challenges of building a truly multicultural society become more difficult in our own country and elsewhere, it is becoming increasingly fashionable in some academic and public policy circles to propose approaches based on models of "separate development" or "parallel communities."

In my view, confronting the myth of separateness, asserting our relatedness – speaking truth to power, as the Quaker principle puts it – is the first step towards resolving conflict and creating peace. My favourite definition of conflict draws from this dynamic.

> Conflict is a crisis that forces us to recognize explicitly that we live with multiple realities and must negotiate a common reality; that we bring to each situation differing – frequently contrasting – stories and must create together a single shared story with a role for each and for both.[2]

This definition requires, first, that we recognize the basic truth that there *is* a conflict, even a crisis, in a given situation. You may be happy to know that the Chinese authorities have now fully recognized and made peace with the mummies of Xinjiang – and have turned them into a major tourist attraction.

Although each of us is different and special, I believe there is much more that binds us together than divides us. Another recent archaeological finding suggests this is not just a personal belief, but is actually true. It turns out that all aboriginal cultures of the northern hemisphere have looked at the constellation we know as Ursa Major and have recognized in those stars the image of a bear. The Innu and Haida of North America, the Celts and Lapps of Europe, the Mongols of Central Asia and the Ainu of Japan – all of these disparate peoples have shared a particular vision of themselves and of the cosmos.[3]

Some scholars theorize that we began to lose this shared human imagination about 7,000 years ago, when the predominant symbol of human society began to shift from mother bear and cub, to wolf and pack, representing a shift from a society based on on intimate relationship, to one based on a collective structure. Today, when I look up at those same stars, I can only pick out the smaller group we know as the Big and Little Dippers – the larger constellation, the bear, completely eludes me.

But our ancestors around the globe, perhaps because they were more closely bound to the natural world and to each other, more rooted in the basic elements of life, were able to look from different perspectives and to see something in common, and even to share an understanding as one people. Now, I think that's truly something special!

---

[1] See Xinhua News Service, "Dozens of Well-Preserved Mummies Found in Xinjiang," February 26, 2001. For a brilliant analysis of textile archaeology in Central Asia, see also Elizabeth Wayland Barber, *The Mummies of Urumchi* (New York: W. W. Norton & Co., 1999).

[2] David Augsburger, *Conflict Mediation across Cultures: Pathways and Patterns* (Louisville: Westminster John Knox Press, 1992).

[3] Paul Sheppard and Barry Sanders, *The Sacred Paw: The Bear in Nature, Myth and Literature* (New York: Viking Penguin, 1985).

6 Light

Darkness and light, hatred and compassion. The past month has served me with a stark reminder of what radically different experiences constitute our world. And I have been reminded of how desperately urgent it is, as our paths inevitably and increasingly cross in this global village, that we ensure that these meetings are opportunities to share our lives, rather than for our worlds to collide.

My first journey took me to Yemen, an ancient, impoverished country occupying a remote corner of the Arabian Peninsula, across the Red Sea from Somalia and the other forgotten countries of the Horn of Africa. I had been asked to chair an international conference to address the difficult legal and human rights issues represented by the thousands of people being held arbitrarily and indefinitely at Guantanamo Bay, and at a handful of other special detention facilities established by the United States around the Middle East and elsewhere. The conference brought together judges, defence attorneys, and other legal experts, along with a number of the Ministers of Justice from the various countries whose citizens were being held in the "anti-terror" prisons.

The conference was held in Yemen because it was the only country in the region that agreed to grant entry visas to all of the nationalities involved. Sadly, petty rivalries and narrow ideologies continue to prevent people from even speaking with each other – often, the very people who need to be part of creating solutions to the world's problems.

I had been in Yemen once before, about ten years previously, to negotiate a program of human rights reforms with the government – abolition of the use of shackles, an end to arbitrary detention, release of prisoners of conscience, training programs to reduce the customary practice of torture. The authorities had actually followed through on their commitments. Conditions were certainly not ideal, but they were definitely, slowly but gradually, improving.

When I arrived this time, I was met at the airport by a government minister, who had come to welcome me, but also to apologize. Once we were in private, the minister said, "Before the conference begins, I wish to express our regrets that we have betrayed some of the human rights measures we had agreed to when you were last here with us. We are sorry, but we have had no choice. We have been instructed by the United States that if we do not act against the people they suspect, in the way they demand, then we too will be counted as enemies. I personally fear for my life." A minister of state of an independent nation apologizing and sincerely expressing fear of assassination! I was not prepared for this.

The conference had been convened because of the growing crisis resulting from the way that suspected terrorists are being detained and treated. Most of the people held at Guantanamo Bay and at the other facilities were detained in the aftermath of the initial war in Afghanistan, when the Taliban were toppled following 9/11. Some were captured in battle, but many were handed over to the U.S. authorities for the substantial bounty money that was offered at the time. Many of the prisoners may be guilty of terrible crimes, but many may simply have been in the wrong place at the wrong time, or be suffering from the settling of old scores that accompanies any change of regime. Some were children – the youngest only 13 years old.

The question is: will we ever know which is which? More than five years later some 400 people continue to be detained at Guantanamo Bay, and thousands more elsewhere. Many continue to be held in solitary confinement, subject to interrogation methods that include beatings, systematic humiliation, hooding and blindfolding, and the use of dogs, mock executions, and other forms of intimidation and terror. Only a small handful has ever been charged with anything at all, and none have been brought to trial before a legitimate court.

From the outset, the U.S. government had determined that suspected terrorists would not be entitled to the safeguards provided by either international or domestic law. White House officials even declared that the purpose of the detentions was vengeance and punishment, rather than truth and justice, and that due process and respect for human rights were therefore not required. Prisoners were refused even the

right of *habeas corpus* – the foundation of all due process
since the Magna Carta in 1215 – and were to be judged by
special military tribunals appointed by the president, which
had the power to impose the death penalty and whose decisions were not subject to appeal.

The critical thing about "human rights" is that they
are supposed to apply to everyone, equally, and always –
especially in times of uncertainty and crisis when people
are most vulnerable to discrimination. This is not a matter
of political niceties or legal technicalities. At stake are the
basic human rights we all depend on – and take for granted:
the right to be presumed innocent, to have legal counsel and
to challenge the legitimacy of your detention before a judge,
the right not to be tortured, the right to let your family know
that you are alive. In deciding that certain people are not
entitled to these fundamental "rights," the U.S. government
has actually determined that certain people are not entitled
to be considered "human."

This should worry all of us, because if it can happen
to some people, then we *all* become vulnerable to the arbitrary judgement and unrestrained will of the powerful. It is
vital that we in the West understand that for many people
throughout the Islamic world, perhaps most, this has been
heard clearly as a message directed at all Muslims. I was
quite overwhelmed to discover how virulent and deep are the
feelings of bitterness and hatred toward us, which have been
fomented among the peoples of the Middle East as a result
of Guantanamo, Abu Ghraib, and other actions that have led
people to feel that we do not respect or even recognize their

human dignity. The arbitrary detentions and unfair trials of Guantanamo are yet further provocations that serve only to deepen resentment and stimulate terrorism.

When I went to Yemen, I had no idea how profoundly abusive the arbitrary detention system is, or how widespread its impact. My own ignorance points to what is perhaps the most worrying aspect of this situation. In my experience, no matter what the controversy, most ordinary folk are well able and willing to distinguish between the particular policies of the U.S. government, and the general attitudes of the American people. As part of the conference, we met with representatives of more than 60 families of detainees, from various countries, in addition to the jurists. I was struck by how they were much less inclined to make any distinction between us, as *citizens* of Western countries, and the policies of our governments, precisely because it is increasingly apparent to them either that we are determined not to know what is going on, or that we simply don't care.

Terry Waite, the British hostage negotiator who himself spent almost five years as a hostage in Lebanon, worked with me during the conference, especially meeting with the relatives. Afterwards he said, "I know what it's like to have no rights. My family knows what it is like to have no information about me, even whether I am alive or dead. There are many families around the world who are in this same

position now because of Guantanamo Bay. You do not defeat terrorism by adopting the methods of terrorists. There will be no moral ground on which we can stand if we allow this to continue. They are simply creating more terrorists."

One of the outcomes of the conference in Yemen was a decision to challenge before the U.S. Supreme Court the legality of the detention process and of the military tribunals. It took a couple of years to work through the system, but eventually both appeals were successful. President Bush's response was simply to adopt a new law, the Military Commissions Act of June 2006, which suddenly made "legal" everything the Supreme Court had just ruled was unacceptable.

The system represented by Guantanamo Bay has been condemned by almost every government and legal authority in the world. Even the UK government of Tony Blair, the United States' main ally in the War on Terror, has denounced it as not only "unacceptable in terms of human rights, but also ineffective in terms of counter-terrorism." To its shame, Canada is one of the few countries that have chosen to remain silent, even though one of the inmates is a Canadian citizen (Omar Khadr, a young man who was only 15 at the time of his arrest).

Created and carried on in the name of defending democracy and advancing freedom, Guantanamo Bay and the other institutions of the War on Terror are part of a perverse system of profound abuse that undermines the moral integrity and political credibility of our nations. We play fast and loose with our principles to our own peril. Guantanamo Bay stands as an open sore on our body politic, a fundamental

contradiction of the commitment to human rights and respect for the rule of law that is the lifeblood of democracy. If
the cynicism and corruption it breeds is not dealt with, the
infection will spread until the host itself is threatened.

On returning from Yemen, I was invited to attend the
Vancouver "Roundtable Dialogue" of the Dalai Lama; Des-
mond Tutu; and Shirin Ebadi, the 2003 Nobel peace laureate
from Iran. Though I carried a heavy heart into the meeting,
it turned out to be a wonderful day of insight and nurture, of
shining examples of the commitment to the way of peace and
understanding. I had met the Dalai Lama and Archbishop
Tutu on several previous occasions, and I was most eager to
hear professor Ebadi, who continues to face daily and intimately the struggles of life and the threats to human rights
in the Middle East.

Ebadi seemed to speak directly to the sense of despair I
had come with that day: "What is important is to nurture day
after day your relationship with the Creator of the universe.
It is in opening our hearts to God that our lives and work become purposeful, and not just the creation of more problems.
This is the path to human salvation: to discover and focus
on that which we share and which brings us together, and to
leave aside those things which separate and divide us."

Darkness and light, hatred and compassion. This is a
time when the world needs all of us as ambassadors of hope
and commitment.

7 Words

Simon Winchester, a British journalist who spent much of his career in Asia, has recently published a history of the making of the Oxford English Dictionary.[1] The OED was one of the great imperial projects of the Victorian age, part of the cultural movement that accompanied the emergence of the great European nation states in the 19th century.

The masters of empire were instinctively attracted to grand projects inspired by a desire for permanent and authoritative structures. This no doubt enhanced their sense of control over their worlds. But unlike similar projects that were launched in France, Germany, and Italy at about the same time, the OED did not attempt to set out the complete vocabulary of the language, nor to draw the boundaries of what should be considered pure or proper English. Its compilers did not even propose a mechanism for determining which words would be "officially permitted" by those who considered themselves to be "the great and the good" of society.

Instead of compiling a definitive list of words and es-
tablishing their fixed meanings, the men and women who
created the OED saw themselves as writing a biography of
each word, charting the way meanings shift and develop
over time depending on context and perspective. They understood the English language as something continually
growing and changing, shaped by the different experiences
and circumstances of the people who speak and write it. I
was reminded of this reality recently, when one of my sons
described a piece of music as "totally sick" – meaning that he
thought it was "very good."

I guess there is still a bit of the old imperialist in me, in
that I sometimes rankle at this fluidity of meaning; there's
something in me that seems inevitably to sit a little uncomfortably in the midst of ambiguity. I remember my first
visit to Africa many years ago. Travelling in the company
of a wise Congolese scholar, I was having a hard time understanding what was going on in the negotiations we were
conducting, especially figuring out the roles different people
were playing in different settings. Finally, the old man said
to me, "My friend, in Africa, identity is contextual. First try
to understand deeply the situation; then try to listen deeply
to the person." Perhaps it is a matter of being well grounded
in the fundamental realities of life, while not being bound in
our particular approach to them.

In searching for the origins of words, the creators of
the OED discovered that, of course, there is no such thing
as "original" English. Every word derives from some source
drawn from the accidents and designs of history, the residue

of a chance encounter with a visitor or an invader, or the souvenir of some special journey or shipwreck survivor. In the course of their research, the creators of the OED discovered that the most ancient words in the English language are these: dirt, earth, root, hearth, star, spirit. I'm not sure why, but I find something quite wonderful in that.

Perhaps it is because, again, it seems like more than simply a collection of words. Taken together, these words seem to describe a set of relationships, or to point toward a fundamental truth, a sense of what is enduring in the midst of a changing world. They point us, literally, to the real grounding of our lives, to what is essential in order for us to feel at home in the world.

One of my favourite philosophers, Simone Weil, was active in the French resistance movement during World War II. Just before the D-Day invasion, she was commissioned by General De Gaulle to prepare a proposal on the spiritual principles that should guide the rebuilding of the nation after liberation. She titled the book she wrote in response to this request *L'Enracinement*, "the need for roots."

For many years I thought of myself as a "seeker" – a seeker after truth, after justice, after love, even after God. Today, reflecting on that list of ancient words, I realize I am no longer comfortable with that notion of being a "seeker." It seems to suggest that those treasures – truth, justice, love, even God – can be found somewhere "out there" – as if truth may be discovered in an idea, or as if justice can be captured in a law, or as if love depends on another person, or as if God can be encountered in a belief.

A few weeks ago, my wife and I caught a performance of the Cotton Patch Gospel down at the Dream Café. It was a powerful presentation, and I was particularly struck by the part of the play where the Jesus character says something like, "Don't keep looking somewhere else for the holy or sacred in life – start looking right around you, and within you. Don't keep thinking it's somewhere off in the distant future – it's right here, right now. Explore it!"

That seems to be one of those "lessons" it takes me forever to learn, but it sounds good. Maybe I'll try thinking of myself not as a seeker, but as an *explorer.*

---

[1] Simon Winchester, *The Meaning of Everything: The Story of the Oxford English Dictionary* (New York: Oxford University Press, 2003).

8 Audit

When it comes to politics, I like to think I am principled but not partisan. I have definite leanings, to be sure, but I'm fickle and don't like to be taken for granted. Although my voting record would not exactly make for much of a rainbow, it would reflect at least a somewhat colourful spectrum – a liberal splash of red, an independent streak of orange, a healthy fringe of green. I have lived long enough to be suspicious of any ideology and to know that truth, like its opposites, can be found in many places – usually in bits and pieces on all sides.

Like most people, I was somewhat shocked and outraged by the government waste and corruption exposed by the report of the Federal Auditor General delivered last February. Since then, the Auditor General has issued two further audit reports – one on the inadequacies of quality control systems related to agricultural industries, I think; and the latest on the shortcomings of airport security and other anti-terrorist measures.

I have a great deal of respect for the work of the Auditor General, and I hold the principle and practice of accountability very highly as a value in personal, professional, and organizational life. However, I must admit that when the latest audit report came out, I began to feel a little weary of the criticism levelled against the government. After all, most of the work of a government is carried on not by politicians, but by civil servants. And most of them are people who, like me and probably like you, try to do a reasonably good job, carry a sense of public service, and want to make a positive contribution in the world. Sometimes, they also make mistakes – like me and probably like you.

No doubt governments make many serious mistakes and even commit acts of deliberate wrongdoing, and certainly those responsible need to be held to account. At the same time, I am sure there must be much in the daily endeavours of the public sector that we should recognize and celebrate as creative, dedicated, and effective work. I wonder what would happen to the political culture of our country if we affirmed at least one success story for every ten cases of failure dissected in our audit reports.

I don't propose focusing on positive developments simply to make us feel good about ourselves, or as some cheery effort to look at the "bright side." Nor am I suggesting that we ignore the failures. I simply am not confident that "learning from our mistakes" is always an effective approach when it comes to making positive change. I believe that the main things we learn from focusing on failure are how to make excuses, how to apportion blame, and how to avoid responsibility. These may be valid survival tactics, especially in the cut and thrust of seeking political advantage. But they tend not to help us learn how to thrive in our relationships, or to move forward together as a community.

I've become convinced that it is more important to try to lift up and learn from our successes, to draw lessons and energy from our positive experiences that can be applied to the many other situations that need them. I believe that just as we learn more powerful and effective lessons from success than we do from failure, so we build more dynamic communities and more productive organizations by recognizing our assets and by working from our strengths, than we do by being preoccupied with our weaknesses and threats. Shifting our approach in this way might even help us develop a healthier approach to accountability.

Accountability is central to any position of responsibility or authority, but it usually only presents itself as a concern when there is a major problem or failure. We tend to associate accountability either with reporting to our bosses, or with knowing whom to blame when something goes wrong. As a discipline of leadership in community, however, accountability should mean much more than having your finger ready to point, or your letter of resignation handy.

We should insist that our political leaders model accountability as a proactive and constant practice, as something expressed not just "up" the hierarchy, but in all directions. As community members, we might *all* ask ourselves, "What can I do to show that I am part of a collective team serving a common purpose?"

9 Diefenbaker

As far back as I can remember I've been a "political junkie." My best Christmas ever was when I was five years old, and my grandmother gave me 12 hats as a present – cowboy, police, firefighter, construction worker, etc. – all the standard options for boys at the time. After several hours of intensive play "trying on different hats," my grandma asked, "So what do you think you'll want to be when you grow up?" Family lore has it that I considered this for a moment, and then answered, "Prob'ly a diplomat." Yes, I think my parents were quite concerned! No doubt they hoped it was something that I'd grow out of in time, like a childhood allergy.

In fact, my condition only got worse. When I was ten and growing up in Montreal, my best friend, Brendan, and I got into a deep political argument. It was the 1960s – a turbulent time, with many of the issues familiar to us today: minority governments, rising nationalism in Quebec, and trade and military tensions between Canada and the United States. Lester B. Pearson had just taken over the government from

John Diefenbaker. I wish I could recall what our dispute was about, but it has completely disappeared from my memory. I *do* remember that Brendan and I agreed it needed to be dealt with urgently, and that it could only be settled by referring the matter to the Prime Minister.

The next day we skipped school, somehow managed to get on a train to Ottawa, and made our way to Parliament Hill, busy all the while with our debate. I think it was only when we actually walked up the steps under the Peace Tower and entered the vast dark lobby that we realized what we had done. Or maybe it was because it was lunch time and we were suddenly hungry. In any case, we'd become runaways, on our own and without a penny in a strange city. Our desperate imaginations ran far ahead – we'd never be able find our way home again and no doubt would be lost forever. We sat down on a cold stone bench in a shadowy corner outside the House of Commons and tried to figure out what to do. The best option seemed to be to simply burst into tears.

Suddenly a jangle of bells rang, doors flung open, and the lobby filled with the commotion of what seemed like hundreds of jostling men in suits, loudly laughing and arguing with each other. They were far too preoccupied with themselves and the importance of their own business to notice the two children cowering in the corner. Except, that is, for one tall man with wavy grey hair and large jowls, whom we recognized immediately as "Dief the Chief." He marched over purposefully, glared down, pointed an accusing finger at us, and demanded, "Why aren't you boys in school?"

We blurted out our confessions while Mr. Diefenbaker listened and nodded gravely. He then summoned an assistant, took us for lunch, and arranged for our safe return to Montreal. Before sending us off, he gave us "the speech." This involved making us promise that we would never skip school again, and telling us that to be good citizens, regardless of what profession we chose to follow, we must study hard and develop skills that would allow us to "serve the people."

I don't remember much else about "the speech." In the years since, I have met many individuals who had an encounter with Mr. Diefenbaker when they were young. I once shared an apartment with someone who drove for four days from Alberta to Ottawa when he was 18 years old, to knock at Prime Minister Diefenbaker's door for advice. It seems we all received the same speech, though the only part of it anyone remembers is the phrase "study hard so you can serve the people."

What we remember more clearly is that this important leader actually noticed us, made time for us, treated us seriously, and made us feel that we really mattered and had something valuable to contribute to our country. Few of us today could name a single policy or program that marked Mr. Diefenbaker's time in office, but each of us who met him identify it as one of the most inspiring and influential moments in our lives.

In so many ways, we live in very different times. In these days of obsessive "national security," it is no longer even imaginable that a couple of children could wander into the

House of Commons – or perhaps even that they would want to! Yet I suspect that the fundamental social needs of young people – to feel that they are part of a community, to be recognized and treated with respect, to believe that they are needed and valued, to be inspired – have not changed all that much.

During the past month of election campaigning and debates, I have found myself less and less interested in the personal competitions and policy controversies presented as priorities by the different political parties. I've invested less and less effort in weighing the merits of which party would spend more or less of our money on the health system or on child care, or how many "free votes" they would give to members of parliament.

Instead, I've become increasingly concerned with questions of leadership, character, and citizenship. I find myself remembering lunch with Mr. Diefenbaker, and the simple fact that this man in a lofty position was grounded enough to actually *see* me and my friend, and to know that something was wrong.

I've tried to picture our current leaders in this situation. Which of them would be most likely to notice a lost child in a crowd, to take personal responsibility for their safety, to make space in their busy schedule to have a serious conversation with them, and to speak with them *sincerely* about the value of "serving the people"? My sense is that those are the political qualities we'll need, if we are truly to begin to address the "democratic deficit" in our country.

10 Monkey

Some years ago, I stayed with a village of tribal people who lived deep in the tropical rainforests of an island off the coast of Southeast Asia. Their lives were very local and traditional in most respects, except for one aspect of their economy. A major portion of their cash income was gained by capturing exotic monkeys for zoos and for other collectors all over the world. I was not particularly happy about that practice, but that's another story. What most intrigued me was the way they captured these intelligent and elusive animals.

The method was elegant in its utter simplicity. First, the people would make a trap by weaving a basket in the shape of a large jar. The basket had a very narrow opening at one end, just large enough for the monkey to squeeze its hand through. This basket trap would be tied to a tree, and a piece of fruit dropped inside as bait. The people would then hide in the undergrowth and wait. If they were lucky and quiet enough, before long the hunters would see one of the small, rare monkeys drop from the trees and cautiously approach the basket.

Once the monkey had reached inside the basket to grab the bait, the hunters would jump from the bushes and run toward the trap with a net. The monkey would instantly leap to escape, only to find itself held by the trap and unable to get away. Of course, the means of liberation was readily "at hand." The only thing actually holding the monkey was the fact that its hand was clenched around the bait – if the monkey had relaxed its grasp and released the piece of fruit, it could easily have slipped its hand free of the trap and have escaped. Yet the monkey almost never did this. It was almost always caught, and the hunters carried home their struggling prize to a happy celebration of their success.

When I first saw this practice, I thought that the effectiveness of the trap had to do with the size of the bait, but, after a while, I realized that it really made no difference whether it was a large banana or something the size of a cherry. In fact, theoretically, the trap would have worked just as well if there was no bait at all, because it depended entirely on an attitude of mind reflected in the monkey's fist – an insistence on clinging onto something, which, however desirable, is a threat to one's freedom, well-being, and even one's very survival.

On that island, I began to learn some important lessons, in particular about forgiveness. I learned, for instance, that forgiveness is not something we do for others, but something we do for ourselves. It sounds obvious, but if you are a person like me, who likes to hold onto their feelings of righteousness and resentment when bad things happen, letting go is actually quite a challenge. Ginn Fourie, whose young daughter was killed in an apparently pointless terrorist bombing in South Africa in the 1990s, has described forgiveness as choosing to set aside and let go of a person's sense of having a legitimate right to revenge.

It is often hard to let go of certain things, both as individuals and as a culture, even when we know that they trap and block us from living as the healthy persons or communities we want and have the potential to be. It may be a possession, a preconception, or a prejudice we have; perhaps it is a behaviour or a self-concept. Perhaps it is an attitude such as cynicism, which prevents us from trusting or even recognizing good in others. Perhaps it is a habit, such as persisting in devotion to institutions or relationships that are not trustworthy. Perhaps it is investing in notions of security that have nothing to do with real safety or well-being. Often it can simply be fear.

Whatever it is we find difficult to let go of, it is usually easier to recognize it in others. For example, it seems easy for us, as Canadians, to see clearly the obsessive and self-destructive actions of our neighbours in the United States, as they doggedly pursue an unattainable sense of safety by investing unimaginable amounts of their resources in space-based weapons, or in the blind and vengeful lashing out that is the war Iraq.

At the same time, as we seem to find ourselves facing another election, reflecting on what kind of a country we want to be, we would do well to pay attention to the ways in which our own political leaders may invite us into places of fear or entrapment. Perhaps this should be a time for us to reflect on and engage in the work of forgiveness – identifying and letting go of the burdensome false notions that we hold onto, and that stand in the way of our freedom, well-being, and survival – of living the fullness of life that we are called to.

11 Sockeye

I had a profound experience recently that filled me with a powerful and tangible sense of hope. I guess that makes it, by my definition, a spiritual experience.

Early one morning about two months ago, something happened that a lot of people would never have dreamed possible. The event took place beside Shingle Creek, where it enters the Okanagan River Channel on the Penticton Indian Reserve. Soon after sunrise, people from all parts of the community began to gather. Before long there were hundreds of people milling about – old friends in conversation, newcomers being welcomed, special guests from up and down the valley, children playing in the water.

The gathering was the culmination of the hard work of many people from throughout the South Okanagan. During the previous five years, they had laboured to restore the quality of the water and the condition of the creek beds in this part of the valley. On the bank above the creek, a group of spiritual leaders from the Okanagan First Nation began to drum and to sing a special song of celebration and encouragement.

A government truck arrived, and, surrounded by the crowd, backed as close as it could to the creek. Children, parents, elders, and youth then formed a long, human chain from the road, down the steep bank, and into the rushing stream. From hand to hand, bucket after bucket was passed down the line. Each one was filled to the brim with leaping silver – hundreds of glistening sockeye salmon fry!

Sockeye have not been seen in the Okanagan water system for at least 50 years, but that morning more than 350,000 tiny salmon swam from the buckets lowered gently into the creek.

The plan is that the salmon fry will spend the next year growing strong in Skaha Lake before they set out on their journey to the sea. Then, *if they* survive, and *if we* keep working together and doing the things we need to do to clean up and protect the environment, four years from now the sockeye will return to the Okanagan. If all goes well, 12 years from now the cycle of life will be restored, and salmon will again spawn in Shingle Creek.

Hopefully! Twelve years is a long time to wait in hope; too bad we didn't start earlier. Then again, as the ancient teaching goes, "The best time to plant a tree was 20 years ago, the second best time is now."

I asked someone for a translation of the song the Okanagan spiritual elders were chanting and drumming to the salmon fry that morning. The words were more elegant and complex than I can reproduce, but essentially they were a combination of, "Welcome back, Salmon! Grow strong, swim fast! Hopefully! If we do the work!"

I came away from Shingle Creek that morning with a real sense of joy, and every time I pass along the river channel I can't help but smile. I felt as though I'd been awakened. I remembered the advice of a therapist on how to deal with insomnia – to call to mind the best thing that happened to you that day, and to analyze why it happened. Perhaps that approach applies not only when one is trying to sleep, but when one is trying to be fully awake. The event at Shingle Creek reminded me of the importance of being attentive to signs of hope in our lives, and of nurturing this as an essential and practical discipline in the work of creating a just and sustainable future. It also reminded me that the best places to look for signs of hope is where people are actually working together, doing something to bring about change, however small or simple.

Something happened that day. In truth, it was just a small thing, a sincere but tentative effort in the face of the seemingly overwhelming challenges confronting our planet. Tiny salmon slipped from our fingers into the water. Dazed by the sun and shocked by the cold rush of the creek, they hesitated for a moment before searching out their unimaginably perilous journey down the Columbia River and into the Pacific Ocean.

And yet, somehow it seemed to be an act of enormous significance, a timeless moment when we glimpsed the real meaning of possibility, the fragile but irrepressible power of life seeking life. Perhaps there is no such thing as a *small* act of hope.

12 Harvest

I love driving into Naramata on Old Main Road, especially at this time of year. There is a beautiful apple orchard alongside the stone wall just before you come down to the big bend by the lake. It has a wonderful mix of red and golden delicious fruit, and, as harvest time approaches, I think of it as the Okanagan equivalent of the splendid turning of the leaves in the maple forests of Quebec, where I grew up.

Another thing I love about harvest time is the way it brings communities together. Well, naturally – have you ever tried to harvest on your own? Harvesting is more the stuff of choirs than of soloists! Maybe if you have a very small garden you can do all the picking by yourself, but I'll bet even then there is a lot of sharing going on – spare squash and zucchinis handed over the fence, a bouquet of gladioli for the altar in the community church, jars of jam and chutney sent to friends and family with a hand-written label and a special slip of ribbon.

About 30 years ago, I learned that if your garden is at all large you will need other people to help with the harvest. Back then, I was a member of a small community of young people who operated a "House of Hospitality" in Griffintown, a very poor neighbourhood in downtown Montreal, where the refuges from the Irish potato famine had originally found a new home. A century and a half later, our community continued to provide food and shelter to the homeless, and operated a community centre, which offered support for the children and families of the area. At that time, harvesting was a very urban thing for us, as we went out in teams early every morning to scrounge food from dumpsters at the commercial markets!

Late one summer our friends Jim and Anne, "back-to-the-landers" with five small children on a 200-acre farm, sent an urgent appeal to our community to help them bring in their harvest. A couple of us who had never even been on a farm before were sent deep into rural Quebec, with the notion that we might also find there an opportunity for a bit of rest and renewal in the peaceful countryside.

On the first day, I was given an antique two-handed scythe and introduced to a 15-acre hay field. I have never in my life, before or since, been as utterly exhausted as I was that first week. It didn't matter that the farm had no electricity, because every evening I was fast asleep long before the sun went down. One day I actually fell asleep with my face in my supper plate!

When I wasn't feeling exhausted, I was feeling overwhelmed and way, way over my head. I realized that I had come to the farm knowing absolutely nothing about harvesting. I certainly hadn't appreciated how much hard, physical work it takes to support and sustain us every day. But I learned all that – especially about perseverance and the importance of working together on things that matter. We got that hay mown and, with the help of an old horse named Buckingham, we even managed to get it raked, cured, and put away in the barn. We also picked and preserved a lot of vegetables and churned many pails of cream.

That winter was cold and harsh, but we had the comfort of knowing that the work we did probably made the difference in helping Jim, Anne, and the children make it through to another spring. And every month or so, a package would arrive on our bitter, windswept doorstep in the city – hefty beef roasts, rich rounds of cheese, and sparkling jars of red and yellow preserves – sweet farm treats for our winter soup-kitchen.

I've always thought that the Jewish calendar got it right by celebrating the New Year (Rosh Hashanah) at the beginning of harvest season. May we all have a great year and a plentiful harvest to share. And may we enjoy harvesting together!

13 Sometimes

November has arrived in a gloomy fashion this year. The rains have come, and have stayed. We've even had a shock of snow.

Maybe it's the influence of the weather, but there also seems to be a sense of foreboding in the air – a heavy mixture of grief and anxiety. Some of us have attended too many funerals recently for friends and for neighbours who have died far too young. As I write, the smoke is still rising on the hillside across the lake, from the pyres on the Penticton Indian Reserve. And rusty red tinges that are beginning to appear among the ponderosa pines along the ridge bear warning that the forests of our little valley will not be spared the sweeping devastations of global warming.

The news reports from the wider world are sombre and sobering. People all over the world seem to be sharing this preoccupied mood. The tragedy of Darfur grinds on month after month, the refugees reaching out to an international community that seems unable to offer either conviction or response. Israel and Palestine lurch from one bitter crisis to the next, the raging cycle of violence and retribution held in motion by a seemingly endless reserve of fear and despair.

And, as if underlying it all, the occupation and destruction of Iraq continues to squander the resources and betray the aspirations of an entire generation. It is not only the 94 civilian lives this outrageous and illegal war claims, on average, every day, that makes it such a moral scandal. Nor is it simply the waste of $2,500 per second that is spent to fan the flames, though this vast sum would be sufficient to put an end to hunger and disease in much of the world. The war in Iraq is a moral scandal because it perversely presumes to do these things in the name of freedom and democracy and because it represents a triumph of the spirit of extremism – the division of the world into "us" and "them." It is a moral scandal because it is guided by an ethic with a single ultimate value: "Those who are not with us are against us... Bring it on."

The war in Iraq represents the acceptance of an approach to exercising power and managing differences that relies solely on the possession of raw power and the arbitrary use of force. If there ever was positive potential in the notion of globalization – such as the possibility that people throughout the world might be able to really participate in sharing information, creating culture, or making decisions – we must now recognize it as simply a system of global domination by the last superpower left standing, what the French call the "Hyperpower."

Of course, every dangerous situation carries within it the seed of a hopeful alternative. I believe that we are always faced with choices and that each of us, together, *can* make a difference, though doing so is often difficult. It can be hard to sustain such a belief, but sometimes it actually happens. Nelson Mandela probably symbolizes this reality most fully. A person with every reason not to, he nevertheless had the vision, courage, and grace to choose a different path and to save his country from war. A lot seems to hang in the balance just now. It will be hard work to help our leaders understand and embrace the responsibility of their power. But sometimes...

A few years ago, on a grim November day much like this one, I was crammed together with hundreds of other people on an underground train in London. We all struggled to maintain our balance and patience – not to mention dignity – as the train pitched and squealed, lurched and then stalled. The lights flickered for a few moments and then when out altogether. The strange silence of controlled anxiety settled on us in the darkness.

Eventually, the emergency power kicked in, and the reserve lights blinked on. In the dim glow I noticed a poem on one of the advertising posters above the dark windows. I jotted the poem down, and for a while I carried it in my wallet. It seems that most years around this season I find myself looking for that scrap of paper.

I found the poem again and thought I'd share it with you – just in case you feel like you're on an underground rollercoaster these days, casting about and out of control; or

like you're stuck within the strained silence of a dark cave.
It goes like this.[1]

Sometimes things don't go, after all,
from bad to worse. Some years, muscadel
faces down frost; green thrives; the crops don't fail.
Sometimes a man aims high, and all goes well.

A people sometimes will step back from war;
elect an honest man; decide they care
enough, that they can't leave some stranger poor.
Some men become what they were born for.

Sometimes our best efforts don't go
amiss; sometimes we do as we meant to.
The sun will sometimes melt a field of sorrow
that seemed hard frozen; may it happen for you.

---

[1]   Sheenagh Pugh, *Selected Poems* (Bridgend, Wales: Seren Books, 1990). Sheenagh Pugh's poem is reproduced here with the special permission of the author, a Amnesty International member, and her publisher.

14 Normal

Some years ago, in Toronto, I found myself in a situation where I had to ask for directions. Yes, I suffer from this notorious, apparently gender-based difficulty – the reluctance to ask for help.

The only person around was in a wheelchair and evidently suffered from a severe neurological disorder, though the man was on his own and clearly able to function independently. Nevertheless, I remember looking around to see if there might be anyone else I could possibly ask for help.

I wasn't really aware of all the judgements and assumptions I was making about this man, until I came closer to him and saw the button he wore on his jacket. It read simply, "Who is normal?" Three silent words, but it was as if they screamed at me from a giant billboard.

In the 30 years since that experience, I've found the question "Who is normal?" to be one of the most useful and challenging we can ask, both as individuals and as a society. One of the current places where this challenging of assumptions might be helpful is in relation to the issue of same-sex marriage. A recent mailing I received from my Member of Parliament reports that the vast majority of people who responded to his poll strongly hold the opinion that the term "marriage" should apply exclusively to the so-called traditional (too often a code word for "normal") relationship involving a man and a woman.

I've tried to follow the arguments on this issue carefully, but I must confess that I've never understood the basic objection to extending "marriage" to same-sex couples. The notion that marriage is an "institution" that needs to be restricted to certain legitimate (often another code word for "normal") people seems peculiar to me. Virtually all of the legal aspects of marriage – tax benefits, inheritance arrangements, insurance coverage, even adoption rights – have been recognized for some years in our province as applying equally to same-sex couples.

And after all, "marriage" is first a relationship, and secondly a legal contract. Indeed, on the moral level, if the term "marriage" expresses a set of social standards about the committed character and stability we expect of intimate relationships, then we might think that inclusion of same-sex couples would be seen as a good thing – indeed, even as something to be promoted not simply as a matter of minority rights, but as something generally beneficial to society. Yet it seems that, for many of us, ideological constraints prevent us from looking at issues, or even at each other, outside the strict boxes and rigid definitions we use to fashion our all too often arbitrary and abusive notions of "normal."

A personal example. About ten years ago, in the mid-1990s, Pope John Paul II sent a secret message to the Conference of Catholic Bishops in the United States instructing them to "actively discriminate" whenever possible against gay and lesbian people – such as in cases where they were employed in church institutions, or living in buildings owned by the church.

The letter was leaked to a couple of international human rights activists by one of the American bishops (to his anonymous credit, in my view). As one of the people who received the leak, the thing that struck me most powerfully about the Pope's letter was the justification offered for the abuses he was advocating – that gay and lesbian people were deemed by the Vatican to have an "objective disorder."

This struck me powerfully because it connected to me personally. As a child, I too had been officially categorized by the authorities in the Roman Catholic school I attended as having an "objective disorder." In my case, it was that I was left-handed. In Catholic terminology, an "objective disorder" is an abnormal trait or behaviour that is not necessarily the individual's fault, but which is nevertheless deemed to be "wrong" and to need corrective action. Remember that the word for "left" in Latin is "sinister," and you get a sense of where they're coming from on this.

It seems hard to imagine today, but at that time the fact that I had been identified as having an "objective disorder" authorized teachers to take whatever action they deemed appropriate to correct my "abnormality," even if it involved the use of force or resulted in permanent damage. Until the

1960s, this forcible change of handedness was actually the number one cause of speech impediments in Canada. Since the law was changed to prohibit this abusive discrimination, the proportion of left-handedness in the Canadian population has doubled to more than 20 percent – and continues to increase every year.

Today, most scientists refuse to speculate on what should be considered the "natural" rate of incidence, and left-handedness is increasingly seen as having a number of positive characteristics that enhance the skills and perspectives available to society. Fortunately for me, my parents stood up to the system and insisted that I should be allowed to be, as they put it, "the way God created me." To my mind, that's still the best definition of "normal."

I wrote to the Pope and told him this story. I urged him to accept that such exclusionary notions of "normal" are rarely more than cultural prejudices reflecting the historical ignorance of a particular time and place. As an intelligent man and as a wise leader, I appealed to him to simply and honestly recognize the serious damage these attitudes had done to so many different groups of people over the years, and to do the right thing in relation to gay and lesbian people today.

To my surprise, I actually received a prompt reply! I was informed by the Vatican Secretariat of State that I would be named personally in the Pope's private prayers every day for one week, and that in the meantime I should present myself to the local parish priest for counselling. I was glad of the prayers, but saddened by the arrogance of a mindset that cannot even imagine that a different point of view might

SECRETARIAT OF STATE

FIRST SECTION · GENERAL AFFAIRS

FROM THE VATICAN, 19 November 1992

Dear Mr Evans,

The Holy Father has received your letter and he has asked me to send you this reply.

be possible, even valid. Largely out of consideration for the unsuspecting neighbourhood priest, I declined to take up the offer of counselling.

Who is normal? Either we all are, or none of us are. The terrible devastation visited recently by the tsunami upon communities around the Indian Ocean and on families in so many countries serves as a shocking reminder of how very fragile and precious all of our lives are – irrespective of our class, gender, nationality, and the many other ways in which we may differ. Hopefully, the massive outpouring of compassion and generosity from around the world in response to the tragedy will stand as a measure of the readiness of millions of people to embrace this vision of our shared humanity, and to act on it. May that, too, become an increasing part of what is "normal."

15 Truth

For about 15 years of my life, February meant frantically getting ready for the annual session of the United Nations Commission on Human Rights.[1]

The Commission lasted for about a month, and was held in a vast circular hall at the UN's European headquarters in Geneva – in the great marble palace that used to house the League of Nations. Very little of what happens in the rarefied atmosphere of that cavern of high politics actually finds its way into headlines in our newspapers, even though within it some of the most powerful people in the world address some of the most critical life-and-death issues facing millions of people on this planet.

The vast hall in Geneva contains about 20 rows of desks arranged in ever wider concentric circles. Each desk bears a nameplate of a country or an international organization. Behind each desk sit half a dozen black leather swivel chairs, each wired to provide simultaneous translation in one of the six official UN languages. When things get really boring, you can always turn to watch the translators working in their sound-proof glass cubicles high above the floor, silently enlivening the speeches with the special physical character-istics of their particular language – waving arms (Spanish), facial gestures (French), pointing fingers (Russian), and so on – like mimes at the circus, or big-city traffic cops during rush hour.

Before I attended my first Commission, I had imagined that making a speech at the UN would be a solemn and mem-orable event. It turns out not to be like that at all! Instead, when your turn comes, the president calls your name, you hold up your hand, a red light on your microphone suddenly turns on, and with a slightly trembling voice you present your carefully crafted statement. And it seems like absolute-ly nobody among the thousand or so people in the room pays any attention whatsoever! Conversations continue; traffic flows without interruption. Until you are finished, that is, and then a mob of people crowd around your desk to grab a copy of your text – while the next person on the list attempts to make their speech.

The hall is a pit of constant clamour and mayhem as the real work of "diplomacy" is carried out. Beyond the for-malities, the Commission is actually a festival of hard-core bargaining, high-pressure lobbying, gun-point negotiating, outright arm-twisting, and unholy horse-trading. This is the way the international community "deals" with human rights atrocities. Sound and fury, posture and pretence, the polite trade of official rationales for the official secrets and other "exigencies of state," the embarrassment of truth concealed and confused by much busyness. Occasionally, it decides to do the right thing – though usually for the wrong reasons.

In the years of my experience at the Palais-des-Nations, the great hall fell silent, utterly silent, only once. It felt as if something was terribly wrong. In fact, the entire Commission was held by the crystalline power of a grotesquely disfigured 18-year-old woman seated at the edge of the room. When her turn came to speak, the wrenching sound was like the whole of humanity struggling against all the obstacles in the world; it was as if she was creating human speech for the first time. It was a moment of truth, of testimony, when the words and the body speaking them became one.

A small group of us had conspired to secretly bring this woman, Carmen Gloria Quintana, to the Commission to tell her story. She had somehow, miraculously, survived the unimaginable. We had helped her escape her own country, had brought her to Canada for months of surgery and the nightmare of rehabilitation, and this was her one remaining wish – to tell the world what had happened to her, to her boyfriend, and to the rest of the teenagers in her village in Chile.

Our name was called on the speakers list, the red light flashed on, and Carmen began to speak, rasping out the words. Slowly, the room gradually hushed, as precisely, scientifically, she described the plain, cruel facts of her experience. How General Pinochet's soldiers attacked her poverty-stricken neighbourhood and seized her and her friends. How the soldiers beat them and killed them. How the soldiers threw their bodies onto the rubbish heap, and poured gasoline from five gallon cans over their bodies. How they set fire to them, intending to burn into ash all evidence of the terror, to erase the memory of their lives and suffering as if it were nothing more than a passing whiff of smoke lost in the bright sky of a sunny morning.

As she spoke, the simple mystery of her scars was revealed. From the contorted mouth of a disfigured young woman pulled from the silence of a smouldering pit after the soldiers had gone. The words emerged pure and beautiful and powerful and true. And this revelation compelled silence.

Some say "the truth shall set you free." At that moment, it did not feel much like liberation for anyone in the great marble hall. In our postmodern relativistic world, some say there is, in fact, no such thing as objective truth, only different perspectives. I know that this, at least, is not the case. For in the moment and power of Carmen's testimony before the Commission, everyone there knew they were witnessing the raw presence of truth. Perhaps you know you are in the presence of truth when the only possible response is to be silent.

---

[1] The Commission has now been replaced by the Human Rights Council as a key component of the UN reform program. Hopefully this change will result in more effective protection for the victims of abuses around the world.

16 Sailing

Life is a very unsuitable environment for those who can't stand change or surprises. Things, it turns out, are rarely as they appear at first glance. Even the slightest adjustment of focus or perspective can reveal a completely different world.

The family photo wall in our house includes a number of peculiar images. The news of the past month about the mounting atrocities in Darfur has made me pause on my way down the stairs to look more closely at one of them. It is a photo of me taken about ten years ago, in Sudan. I am sitting awkwardly in a chair made of rough sticks and bits of leather, straining to make a point as I negotiate with a man in a camouflage uniform and red beret.

Examining the photo more carefully recently, I saw something I'd never noticed before. In the background, if you look very closely, you can just pick out the rubble of a recently bombed brick house and, beyond the empty folding chair, a one-legged child. It is as if the boy is balancing like

a tree in the distance. He is the only one looking directly at the camera, and he seems to be waving.

The man in the red beret is Dr. Riek Machar, at the time the leader of one of the main rebel armies that had been waging a war of independence since 1983 against the Islamic government in Khartoum. Unfortunately, the various rebel factions, largely reflecting the different ethnic groups of the southern half of the country, have also spent much of their time fighting each other. In fact, the town of 7,000 where the photo is set had recently been devastated by the forces of Riek's principal rival, John Garang. The three chairs in this picture comprised the entire inventory of non-military "things" – furniture, utensils, tools, food stocks – that remained in the community when I visited. The war had claimed about two million lives at that point.

Sudan is huge, and could be immensely rich. The largest country in Africa, it possesses major oil reserves and a wealth of other resources. It has regularly been described as the "potential bread-basket" of Africa.

It is deceptive. Most of Sudan consists of the supposedly "trackless wastes" of the Sahara desert. But the Nile River flows smack through the middle of the country, and because the land is so flat the immense river slows and spreads wide. The "Sudd," for which the country is named, is actually a swamp that extends for hundreds of miles. A friend of mine did a nutritional study of Sudan in the 1970s and discovered that the major source of protein for several of the Saharan tribal groups is fresh-water fish! Although it looks like endless desert, it sometimes squishes when you step onto it.

Despite the potential riches, the people of Sudan are radically, often desperately, poor. They routinely face starvation, almost entirely because of the war. In the words of Elie Weisel, the Auschwitz survivor and poet laureate of the holocaust, Sudan has become the "world capital of human pain, suffering, and agony."

I had been criss-crossing the war zone for a week, flying with a Danish pilot at about 200 feet in a Cessna borrowed from the UN, searching for Riek and Garang to try to negotiate some agreement to protect civilians. The small plane was stuffed with as many bags of dried food as we could carry, but sure enough, once we found Riek and unloaded the supplies, the plane began to sink into the Sudd. I had 20 minutes to decide whether to leave with the plane or to stay with Riek's army and hope to be picked up again in a couple of days. I sat down with Riek in the shade of a rare tree, and we began our negotiations. Someone took a picture.

The photo was taken early in the afternoon; the real story was yet to unfold. The negotiations were friendly, but inconclusive. The meagre rations we had brought, rice and lentils, was the first real food these people had seen in weeks. As dusk fell, countless small cooking fires appeared across the desert plain, and with the smoke the joyful sound of singing rose into the night.

Then, just as suddenly, the winds rose, the sky clouded over, and torrential rains poured down. One by one the fires were extinguished like delicate candles in the storm, though the singing never stopped. The rain lasted only an hour or so, but the intensity of its brief visit turned the desert into a sea of mud, which meant that it would be weeks before any plane could land and take off again. I could stay and try to tough it out, or accompany Riek and his army to what might be the war's next battle.

We left at midnight, under a bright starry sky, by boat. Five vessels, filled with hundreds of soldiers and prisoners, were assembled at the bottom of a steep bank, where the fast flowing Sobat River, a tributary of the Nile, had carved a trench 50 feet below the desert plateau. The chairs were carried down and placed in the "BGB" – the big green boat in the middle of the flotilla.

We sailed through the night, across the Sahara, arguing and negotiating, as the sentries startled each time a crocodile slid into the waters at our passing. At dawn, we arrived at an understanding, and at Nasir, a town near the Ethiopian

border, and parted to rejoin our separate worlds. Dr. Riek entered into peace negotiations with the government the next
year, and John Garang became the "first vice president" in
the new "government of national unity."

Things are delicate, but at least somewhat hopeful. The
good news is that an agreement has been reached, after 20
years of war, that will allow international peacekeepers to
monitor the truce in the south of Sudan. The bad news is the
continuing failure to agree to anything that will address the
new atrocities taking place in the west of the country – the
Darfur region, where another two million people continue
to be threatened with homelessness and death. One step forward, two steps back? A parsing of suffering, as if that is
a thing some still can tolerate, while the authorities argue
about the legitimacy of the international criminal court and
the definition of genocide.

Setting down the newspaper, I keep returning to the
blurred image of the one-legged child, waving in the background. Or, rather, to change perspective, waving in the
centre of the picture. Beyond the negotiations, beyond the
deceptions and hypocrisies, he stands as an innocent and
precarious reminder of what really matters. A reminder that
a change of focus and perspective has the power to reveal a
different world, a different set of priorities, even a new future. Imagine the possibilities!

17 Shelley

These days, the 19th-century English poet Percy Bysshe Shelley is probably best-known for having been married to Mary, the creator – or at least the author – of *Frankenstein*. Earlier generations knew him more for the romantic energy and revolutionary vision of his poetry, and because they had to memorize it in school! His famous celebration of creativity and hope, "Ode to the West Wind," ends with the wonderful line, "If Winter comes, can Spring be far behind?"

In our less romantic time, preoccupied as we are – and for good reason – more with horror than with hope, more with the pragmatic than with the revolutionary, it seems more appropriate to ask, "If Budgets come, can Elections be far behind?" And given the way that government budgets and announcements appear to be cobbled together and manipulated to serve crude political designs, perhaps it is not so surprising that Frankenstein and his friends are currently more the fashion in our culture.

The voting registration form came in the mail today and, though the election is still months away, the campaign seems already to have burst upon us with full force. It promises to be intense and bitter from beginning to end. Personally, at this point, I have no idea how I will vote when the day comes. I have always been less attracted by the comforts of adherence to ideological "isms" or allegiance to party positions than to the challenge of dealing with real-life questions of values and principles. Perhaps naively, I also like to cling to the notion that my vote is something a candidate must earn from me, rather than something I owe to a party.

As the election gathers around us like the dark storm clouds that bear the heavy rains of spring (sorry, too much Shelley!), there are a number of questions that will guide me as I try to figure out which candidate or party will receive my vote.

Is their vision oriented to the future, or focused on the past?
I don't think Shelley said it, but the old saying is no less true: "You can't stand in the same river twice." However fond our memories of the past may be, anyone whose policies are dedicated to going back or to returning to the way things used to be is probably engaged in some kind of delusion or deception – at least of themselves. As in normal life, such invitations are probably best declined.

Is their vision inclusive?
Every time I hear a party claim to be advocating on behalf of "working families," I wonder about all the people in our com-

munity who are left out of this pithy appeal: retired folks, unemployed people, people on disability, or simply people on their own. I want to know that when a candidate looks around they don't just see, or care about, either their own kind, or those people they think might represent the majority of votes.

Does their campaign express a positive direction?

I want to know if the candidate and their party know more about exercising responsibility, than they know about apportioning blame. Scapegoating is a psychological mechanism by which we make ourselves feel good by making others look bad. It has a well-established function in our organizations, but ultimately it is a negative one. I think any leader who tries to cultivate support by stimulating feelings of fear, anger, or hatred is not trustworthy.

Do they walk the walk?

I don't want to pry into the personal lives of the candidates, but I *do* want to know that they have some real background in community service. After all, that's what it's supposed to be all about, and because of that I look for involvement in more than just their own professional or business association, or trade union. I want to see that the candidate has worked with people outside of their natural circle of self-interest, and that their sense of people's lives is drawn from more than their personal – often very privileged – experience.

Are they willing to speak the truth?

I'm much more likely to trust someone if I can be confident that they are not just trying to tell me what they think I want to hear. It is ironic and perhaps strange, but I find that my ability to trust a leader increases in direct proportion to their willingness to honestly give me the bad news, to openly acknowledge mistakes and to take responsibility for failures, to look for solutions and to admit to not knowing the answer if, in fact, they don't.

Maybe we should conduct some experiments to see if other people experience political trustworthiness the way I do. Who knows, perhaps some day that last point will get dressed up as a formula and come to be known as "Derek's Theorem"! Or, more likely, it will just remind us of the universal truth Percy Shelley captured in one of his less flowery moments: "It is better to keep your mouth shut and appear stupid than to open it and remove all doubt."

18 Dreidel

A dreidel is a traditional Jewish toy, a kind of spinning top. They are usually made of clay or wood, although strangely enough I got a plastic one this year as a "prize" in a Christmas cracker! They are usually decorated with religious words or images, and can be quite ornate. They are, however, a very simple toy.

To make a dreidel work, you hold the top of it tightly between your thumb and forefinger, and then flick it quickly onto the floor or a table. It's all in the wrist action! If you've got the right technique, the dreidel will probably bounce a couple of times, and then spin away in a blur. If it is spinning fast enough, the dreidel will stand straight up, and, for a few precious seconds, will become completely stable. It even seems to spin faster and faster – like a figure skater who draws her arms in tightly and finds that place of perfect balance.

Inevitably, however, the spinning dreidel begins to lose momentum, or stumbles on some small imperfection on the playing surface. Once it begins to wobble, even slightly, it's game over. It cannot recover its balance. The dreidel sways ever more wildly until it crashes. Then it's someone else's turn to try their hand.

The dreidel seems an apt symbol for our historical moment. We achieve a sort of balance for a time, but challenges, contradictions, or a simple loss of energy lead to instability – and a need for initiative and change. The last time the dreidel fell was in 1991, when the Soviet Union collapsed and the Cold War suddenly ended.

Since then we have lived in a very peculiar and dangerous "new world order," in which the direction of global affairs has been set by, and almost entirely in the interests of, the sole remaining superpower. There has been no alternative vision or competing authority to balance, restrain, or refine the political will of the United States. Some scholars have famously referred to this period as "the end of history," in the sense that the critical dialectic that inspires both caution and creativity went into a dormant state. When, in the fullness of time, histories come to be written, I suspect that our current period will be remembered for three significant developments heralding a time of change.

The first has been amply documented: the glaring exposure of America's feet of clay. Despite unprecedented levels of economic dynamism, technological leadership, political authority, and military power, history will nevertheless record that the global position of the United States was foolishly squandered and fundamentally eroded. Driven by a combination of unbridled arrogance, blind vengeance, and profound incompetence, America's unilateral rush into an illegal war in 2002 rapidly turned, by 2006, into a desperate search for means of escape, and a stumbling fall into moral and financial bankruptcy.

The second development future historians will point to is the emergence of China as a fully-fledged superpower. China announced its arrival at the top table in 2005 by confronting Japan, ostensibly over the interpretation of W. W. II history in school texts. Demonstrations erupted in a dozen cities in China to protest the continuing failure of Japan to fully recognize or take responsibility for the atrocities they committed in the region during the war.

No doubt, these protests were organized by the government, and the Japanese started out demanding an apology from the Chinese authorities. But within a few weeks, it was Japan's prime minister who stood to make a formal apology to the whole world. Indeed, that prime minister was soon replaced by a new leader, whose main quality is his dedication to building a positive relationship with China.

Mobilizing and manipulating the masses has been a factor in domestic power struggles in China for decades – Mao being the past master. In this instance, the Chinese authorities showed for the first time that the public opinion of its people is now a political force that can be marshalled for international effect, just as the American government has long been able to mobilize and manipulate domestic public opinion to legitimize or motivate its use of military power around the globe. Foreign leaders are right to stand up to China in support of human rights. As when dealing with any superpower, however, it is best not to do so as either a stranger or as an enemy.

I think the key factor defining superpower status is not primarily money or even military might. Rather, it is whether the opinions of the people of that country truly matter on the international level. The great historian John Lukacs observed that,

> The world is governed, especially in the democratic age, not by the accumulation of money, or even of goods, but by the accumulation of opinions. History is formed by, and politics dependent upon, how and what large masses of people are thinking and desiring, fearing and hating.[1]

Many people during recent years have become disillusioned with traditional politics, especially at the national level, because they felt it offered little opportunity to make a real or effective difference. Concerned citizens increasingly focused their efforts either in their local communities, or at the level of global movements. It was left to ordinary people around the world to form networks, such as the anti-globalization movement or the World Social Forum, to try to express or "constitute" an alternative basis of power.

I believe the third significant development of our time is the growing insistence by the majority of people that they are no longer willing to tolerate political leaders who base their power and priorities on the cultivation of "fearing and hating." If governments continue to ignore or oppose that movement toward a politics based on "thinking and desiring," perhaps it is time that we, ordinary people around the world, figure out how to organize ourselves into a new kind of superpower of our own – one that is less bound by the satisfaction of local interests and more guided by a dedication to solving shared problems.

The good news is that, if Lukacs is correct, we really *can* shape the future. The challenges and obstacles are enormous. But perhaps it is also really quite simple, like picking up a dreidel.

---

[1]   John Lukacs, *Democracy and Populism: Fear and Hatred,* (New Haven: Yale University Press, 2005).

19 Croissant

Last month, I was invited to deliver a set of lectures on religion and human rights at California State University in Los Angeles. The purpose of my visit intrigued the U.S. Customs officer who checked my passport, so he asked about my personal background. After a few details, he leaned back and smirked: "Are you kidding me – philosophy, ethics, human rights? I don't know what you think you're going to do with that in the United States. Philosophy: we ain't got none, and the folks in power at the moment seem to be quite proud of the fact. Ethics: sure, we think that's a good thing, but for other people. As for human rights: well, we can't even spell that anymore. Enjoy your stay in America, sir!"

The lectures were well-attended because, surprisingly, the topic is now relevant. When I was a young man, already a long time ago it seems, I did a university degree in comparative religion. At the time, none of my friends or relatives imagined that this could possibly be the basis for a career – or anything else useful or relevant in the real world for that matter. The study of religion was generally regarded almost as an arcane branch of archaeology; it was seen as an examination of ancient mysteries, which would gradually fade in the face of the powerful mix of scientific technology, free market economics, and Western cultural values that we have come to refer to as globalization.

It was then widely assumed or taken for granted that, on the one hand, universal human rights were an accepted and progressive norm that everyone throughout the world would increasingly support and enjoy, and that, on the other hand, the influence of religion in domestic politics and international relations would gradually decline and eventually disappear. The future, it was thought, would entail some combination of freedom *of* religion and freedom *from* religion. It was generally thought that both of these "trends" – the increase in support for human rights, and the decline of the import of religion – would be good for the health and well-being of the human family. Neither "trend" has played out in reality.

The implication for us today is that we cannot afford the complacent comforts of our past assumptions. We must take both human rights and religion seriously if we are to survive as a species, let alone become a healthy family. It's all about understanding the limits of our individual and social perspectives, and about being dedicated to nurturing real and honest relationships with those we view as the "other," or even as the "enemy."

Coming to grips with the way our assumptions and perspectives can prevent us from seeing reality clearly can be

enough of a challenge! I began the first lecture with a game
of "Where am?" and offered the students four clues:

1. In this country there is one officially recognized state
    religion.
2. All people in this country are deemed to come under
    the authority of this religion, and must pay taxes to
    pay for the salaries of the clerics and for the upkeep of
    the local temples.
3. The head of the government of this country personally
    appoints the chief religious leaders, and they automati-
    cally become voting members of the country's national
    legislature.
4. This country is ruled by a hereditary monarch, who
    swears to defend the official religion against all
    threats.

The students guessed that it must be Saudi Arabia, or some
other Muslim country in the Middle East ruled by a sultan
or an emir. In fact, the correct answer is Great Britain. Of
course, we all know that even if the facts reflected in those
clues are *technically* true, they do not convey an accurate
picture of how real life is actually experienced in the United
Kingdom. We know that there is a lot of nuance and diversity
behind the raw facts, because we are somewhat familiar with
British culture. We know what it's like on the inside.

We know, for example, that even though Anglican bishops are selected by the British prime minister and automatically become members of the House of Lords, few people
really pay much attention to it. We may know, in fact, that

Islam is the majority religion in West Yorkshire, and that overall there are now twice as many Muslims in England as there are regular attendees of the Church of England. We may even know that Prince Charles has declared that, if his time ever comes to be king, he intends to swear to be a "defender of faith," not a "defender of *the* faith." But from the outside, the facts, as I've stated them in the four clues, can appear quite strange and incomprehensible, even offensive and ridiculous.

As with any relationship, outsiders to a religion or culture may be quick to judge it, and are usually much less able to understand it. In today's world, this seems to be especially true of the relationship between Islam and West. Whenever we hear something about Islam that seems incomprehensible or offensive, we should remind ourselves of the importance of perspective – that it may appear strange simply because we are looking at it from the outside.

Our ability to reach mutual understanding is further hampered by that fact that the relationship between Western and Islamic cultures has primarily been that of war – of enemies – for most of the past 1000 years. In the "fog of war," understanding can be hard to find. As the old saying goes, in war "truth is the first casualty." The narrowness of our historical perspective is such that most of us do not even recognize that we have been – or continue to be – at war. Such blindness and forgetfulness is the traditional prerogative of the privileged, of those who are accustomed to being the winners.

The second question I posed in my lecture was, "What is the most significant date in world history?" The students chose 1492, though not because of the event that was considered globally significant at the time, which involved Ferdinand and Isabella of Spain but which had nothing to do with Columbus or America.

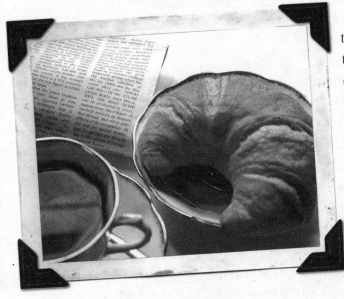

In 1492, the thing that was considered the truly momentous event was the expulsion of the Muslims from Western Europe, after some 700 years of on-and-off fighting. In fact, the Muslims as a political force would not be defeated in Eastern Europe until 1693, when the Ottoman Turks were turned back from the gates of Vienna. This was so significant that a special pastry was invented to celebrate the event. The crescent, *croissant* in French, is the symbol of Islam, as the cross is to Christianity. Biting into a croissant stuffed with ham was originally a very pointed and succinct way of expressing Western attitudes toward the Islamic world!

These events may be the arcane details of a forgotten history, but their impact continues to influence global developments, and even to shape our own lives, whether we recognize it or not.

It is time we recognized it. The wars in Bosnia, Kosovo, Iraq, and Afghanistan need to be understood as simply the latest instalments of our thousand-year conflict with Islam. The careless degradation of Saddam Hussein, the callous desecration of the Qur'an as an interrogation technique, and the cavalier occupation of Muslim territories by Western military forces need to be seen not as isolated incidents but as acts that rise from the deep well of hatred and hostility toward the "other" in our culture. We need to realize that these acts and wars not only inflict terrible suffering on "them," but also increasingly change "us."

The stakes are high. Globalization does not mean some faceless blending of nations into a worldwide cultural conformity. It means, rather, that the repressions, exploitations, and conflicts that may previously have been seen as belonging to a distant "Third World" have become shared realities for communities everywhere.

One of the consequences of the current phase of our war with Islam is that another one of our assumed values, multiculturalism, is increasingly coming under question and threat. More and more communities and nations are abandoning the challenges of dialogue and relationship in favour of a social vision of "separate development" or "parallel communities."

Gaining perspective on the war is not so much a matter of understanding where we have come from, but more and more a question of deciding what we want to become as a nation, as a culture, and as a species.

20 Bells

Hollywood is, sadly in my view, currently filming a "remake" of Alfred Hitchcock's 1963 masterpiece of tension and terror, *The Birds*. Of course, the special effects were rudimentary compared to today's standards, but the emotional intensity of the film was so powerful that the images seared themselves into memory.

Who can forget the sense of menace with which the crows looked down from the electric wires, or the scene of the children running from the school, or the explosion at the gas station? I confess that every time I go into one of those old-style phone booths, with the folding doors, a semi-conscious memory of the film still flashes before my mind, and despite myself I look warily at the sky.

The original movie was filmed a few miles north of San Francisco, in a small coastal community called Bodega Bay, and for years this has been the town's main claim to fame. About ten years ago, however, Bodega Bay began to develop an alternate identity. It, too, is based on a nightmare, but

one that is much more real and ordinary, though no less ter-
rifying, than the one imagined by Hitchcock. It involves the
death of a single child. This alternate, creative new identity is
rooted in the human experience of sorrow rather than in fan-
tasies of terror, and is focused on healing instead of on fear.

In 1994, a seven-year-old boy from Bodega Bay, on a
family holiday in Italy, was shot and killed by highway rob-
bers. It happened out of the blue. In the wrong place at the
wrong time, the family's rental car was mistaken for another one the same colour that was supposed to be carrying
a package of diamonds. I can't begin to imagine the shock
experienced by Nicholas Green's parents as tragedy suddenly
fell with its full weight upon their small family.

Yet in that desperate moment of profound loss and desperate confusion, they somehow found the presence of mind
and generosity of heart to donate their son's organs for medi-
cal transplants. The organs offered new life to seven people,
strangers in a foreign country, including a dying 19-year-
old girl, a blind young mother who had never seen her baby's
face, two children with kidney disease, and a 15-year-old
boy who needed a new heart.

The story became headline news in Italy at the time, both
because of the atrocity and, especially, because of the model
presented by this boy and his parents. People throughout
the country were touched by their ability to consider the
needs of others, even in a moment of extreme loss and need
themselves. The level of organ donations in Italy continues
to be three times what it was before the tragedy. This phenomenon, the way an individual act of courage or generosity

can inspire the same in others, has come to be known as the "Nicholas Effect."

One of the things that especially impressed me was the clarity and frankness with which the Green family addressed the reality of the tragedy they suffered in their lives. "I knew I could never be really happy again," Maggie realized in the moments after her son's death. Reg, the boy's father, has written, "It doesn't take away the emptiness. Nothing I do seems complete anymore. But it does help when I remember that, even in the act of dying, Nicholas saved others in desperate need when no one else could." Reg and Maggie Green acted to transform their loss and suffering into something constructive and beneficial, but it did not make their loss or suffering any less real, or any less permanent.

So often the TV news presents us with the victims of terrible crimes, or their families, emerging in distress from a courtroom and being asked if they "got closure" – as if closure were a commodity one can expect to "get," or something that can be instantly achieved between one moment and the next. Sometimes it is the grieving families or persons themselves who seem to express surprise and disappointment that a verdict or a sentence has failed to "deliver closure," as if it were something one can get from someone else. In these moments, it seems as if the victims are being forced to bear yet another burden – the need the rest of us have to believe that suffering can somehow, even easily, be escaped; a need that we wrap up in a delusional myth called "closure."

I do not believe that there is such a thing as closure when it comes to deep suffering or loss. I believe this notion of closure is too often an abuse foisted on us – and especially on the victims of tragedy and on the survivors of injustice – by our culture of therapeutic consumerism. Several universities are currently researching the development of propranolol, commonly known as the "forgetting drug," meant to prevent painful memories from forming in people who have experienced trauma. The little blue pills are even being envisioned by some as a path to world peace, if administered to entire nations! I am not suggesting that anyone should be forced to endure unending torment from traumatic memories. I am merely saying that we cannot simply ignore or turn the page on suffering or tragedy and expect to find a new life. Instead, we must find ways to acknowledge, embrace, and transform our sense of loss, and to support each other in doing so.

In Bodega Bay, a special kind of memorial has been built to commemorate not only Nicholas, but all children who have been the innocent victims of violence throughout the world. It is a three-metre high scaffold-like structure from which more than 140 bells have been hung: school bells, church bells, ships' bells, mining bells, cow bells – all kinds of bells that have come from all over the world. Reg Green has said that, when the wind blows in off the  sea, the bells chime, "sometimes a few at a time, sometimes an entire orchestra, sounding like happy children at play. Then the sound fades away, and the children are gone."

Einstein revealed to us that energy cannot be truly destroyed or lost to the universe; it can only be transformed

– from matter into heat, from heat into light, and so on. Perhaps that is the purpose of our lives and the real challenge of peace – to remember those who have suffered, to honour them, and to find ways to transform the suffering that they and we have experienced into something that is creative and healing. Traditionally, that's why we ring bells at certain times: to remember, to honour, to celebrate peace, and to dedicate ourselves to creating and preserving it. We need more bells!

21 Gardening

Throughout my life I have built gardens in unlikely places. I have never been terribly interested in the actual gardening itself – the planting and weeding and harvesting and all – but more in the challenge of transforming a piece of barren ground into something that might support beauty and life.

My first garden was in a piece of utter wasteland – the abandoned parking lot of a derelict factory in an area then known as the "grey underbelly" of Montreal. That little patch is still producing flowers and vegetables for the people of that neighbourhood.

A full-page photo of my next garden was actually published in *Harrowsmith* magazine. It was a box garden on the rooftop of a community centre, adjacent to a convalescent hospital. When the hospital staff told us how much the patients enjoyed watching the plants spring up in our collection of old crates and bins, we built an arbour and a boardwalk across the roof to accommodate wheelchairs, so that patients could spend an hour or two in the leafy shade.

My latest project has been transforming an old swimming pool into something I am calling "the fruit pond." I have filled it in one wheelbarrow at a time, and last week it produced its first yellow plum!

For the most part, I have wisely left the work of nurturing seedlings and producing crops to others. Years ago, I learned that the only thing I could reliably grow were roses, largely because they are so independent and determined, and because they even seem to thrive on neglect and adversity. I've always been alarmed by the gardener's advice to "cut back hard." It seems like such a high risk strategy! But sure enough, whenever I've done it, the roses have somehow returned the next year, indomitable and with even greater vigour.

During the past month, I've found myself in two unlikely gardens, in each case witnessing again the fearful vulnerability – and the miraculous resilience – of roses "cut back hard." I spent several days in London before and after the suicide bombings of the buses and the underground. My hotel was just around the corner from King's Cross station, the centre of the attacks.

The first day after the bombings, the crowded streets seemed to be filled with a combination of stunned shock and the typical "grittiness" for which Londoners are so famous. Everyone behaved outwardly as if nothing had happened, despite the disruptions and the constant wailing of emergency sirens. However, by the second day and especially on the third day, strain and emotion began to claw through the veil, as the terrible reality of the atrocity and the persistent nature of the threat settled upon the city.

After a peaceful day of research in the soft natural light and comforting blue leather of the great, round reading room of the British Museum, I walked over to King's Cross to pay my respects at the spontaneous memorial that had sprung up outside the station. This was where the worst of the bombings had occurred, and many of the thousands of commuters and visitors who pass through the station daily had paused to offer a prayer, or a poem, and to lay down some flowers on the sidewalk. There were tributes and messages from people of all cultures and classes, and from all over the world. One of them, scrawled on a scrap of paper and stuck on the grimy brick wall, particularly struck me. It read simply, "Fallen roses, ah, all of them roses."

My travels next took me from London to Central Africa – to Burundi and the Congo – a region that has known immeasurable and seemingly endless terror and atrocity during the past decade of genocide, invasions and civil wars. The war in the Democratic Republic of the Congo, for instance, largely ignored by the world's media and carried on without much public concern, has claimed more lives – some few million, in fact – than any other conflict since World War II.

I was in the region to conduct an assessment of human rights protection mechanisms, and it was tough work. Food was scarce, as were basic amenities; electricity was available only a few hours each day; security conditions were stable, but tense. A 6 p.m. curfew was in effect, and light machine gun fire often disturbed the night. During the day, ranks of ragged, irregular troops would periodically emerge from the mountains and march through the city on their way to a new front-line somewhere to the north.

I've always found the reality of child soldiers deeply troubling. But this time I was shocked at how *many* child soldiers were evident – and by how *young* they were. After a meeting with some officials, I came out of a government building to see yet another line of troops marching along the road. As usual, most of the soldiers had only various bits of uniform, and a chaotic assortment of weapons. I noticed one soldier in particular, a boy who could not have been more than ten years old – perhaps 11 at a stretch. The thing that disturbed me most, though, was not his age, nor even the familiar ease with which he carried his AK-47. It was that he already wore the "hard face" of a veteran, something that cannot be faked.

All was silent as the troops passed. As soon they disappeared around a bend, singing and clapping arose from a house across the way. A wedding was taking place under a veranda. A wise sense of discretion meant that the couple, family, and friends had interrupted their celebration and had disappeared while the hungry troops passed, but now they resumed their festivities with all the joy and splendour they could muster. They even invited the "muzungu" visiting from Canada to join in the celebrations. Just beside the veranda, a large rose bush was in full red bloom. We all gathered in front of it for the photos of the wedding party.

Perhaps there is really no such thing as an unlikely place for a garden. Perhaps every patch of earth – like every aspect of human experience – can be a place of life and beauty, even in places that are "cut back hard." Perhaps the real work of gardening is cultivating our own ability to recognize the beauty that surrounds us, and nurturing our willingness to share life in its fullness.

22 Dream

Loyalty is an amazing thing. Especially the kinds of allegiances that are imprinted on us as children. I was in Los Angeles earlier this year, visiting with a Canadian friend who teaches at a university there. Even though he has always been a hockey fan, I was astonished to find the walls of his office festooned with Montreal Canadiens memorabilia. I should not have been so surprised.

It reminded me of the first time I visited the home of an ex-patriot Canadian when we lived in England. After supper, she asked if I wanted to see something really special, and beckoned me to follow her upstairs to her bedroom. I followed, cautious but curious! There, she went to the closet, and pulled out a shoebox. Carefully, she drew out an autographed photo, dedicated to her, and signed by the Canadiens legendary captain, Jean Beliveau. I was duly impressed.

I was born in Montreal, and lived there through my youth and early adulthood. I went to a high school where really "making it" meant getting to try out for the Habs – i.e., the Canadiens, for those unfamiliar with Canadian hockey teams – an accomplishment that typically was achieved by a member of the graduating class only once every couple of years. As I have moved about the country and around the world in the years since, I have never been able, try as I might, to develop a serious attachment to another team. It makes absolutely no sense, but no matter where I am, and even though I no longer know who any of the players are or where they come from or really even care one way or another, I nevertheless find myself checking the sports pages to see how the Montreal Canadiens fared in their last game!

I've been looking into some family history recently. I come from a very large and vigorous Irish Catholic family. Although we now draw our lineage from Quebec more than from County Clare, Gaelic was still sometimes the language of choice in my grandmother's house, especially if a situation called for a particularly colourful comment. All accounted for, I believe I grew up with more than 70 first cousins – or people referred to as cousins – all within a four-mile radius of my home.

At significant events, such as Christmas or Easter, meals were served in several sittings, by generation – youngest first, elders last. As children, we would conspire to sneak peeks into the elder's meal, certain to be the most boisterous, controversial, and entertaining. There were always people around that table who were referred to as "uncle" or "auntie," but whose actual relation to the family was never entirely clear. One of those people was Uncle Connie, whom we knew was a famous "hockey guy," but whom we were instructed not to "bother with foolishness."

Pretty much forgotten nowadays, Connie Broden has probably been best described as "the answer to one of the best hockey trivia questions ever: Who is the only player to have won the International Ice Hockey Federation World Championship and the Stanley Cup in the same year?"[1]

Uncle Connie had a fabulous year in 1958, the stuff of childhood dreams. He had been a self-described journeyman "fringe player" in the minor leagues for much of his professional career – mostly playing with the Cincinnati Mohawks and the Shawinigan Cataracts. He was finally called up to the NHL by the Montreal Canadiens in the spring of 1957, joining them just in time to play in the final series of the playoffs. He scored one assist, and for his labours had his name inscribed on the Stanley Cup.

The following year he had an injury and played only three games for the Habs, scoring two goals and one assist. The "amateur" team selected to represent Canada in the World Championships that year, the Whitby Dunlops, needed extra players and, as was the tradition, asked for help from the Montreal Canadiens and the Toronto Maple Leafs. Sam Pollock, the General Manager of the Canadiens, primarily concerned about not hampering his team's playoff chances, reportedly fobbed off the request by saying, "Take Broden."

The Dunlops did, and went on to post an undefeated record in the World Championship, outscoring their opponents in the tournament in Norway by 82 to 6, and recovering the gold medal from the Soviet Union. Connie Broden scored in every game, including the tying and winning goals in the final against the Soviets. He was the leading scorer in the tournament – scoring 12 goals and seven assists in seven games. He then managed to return home to Montreal just in time to play with the Canadiens in the final game of the playoffs, and to win his second Stanley Cup!

Uncle Connie retired from professional hockey before the start of the next season; he was 26 years old, and had just graduated from university. In all, he played six games in the NHL, scored two goals and one assist, had a single penalty, and won two Stanley Cups along with a World Championship on the side. Reflecting on his improbable record, he said, "Yes, it was quite a feat when you look back to it. But I was very fortunate. I was a fringe player at best at pro level and I was just lucky to be around when the Canadiens won the Cup. But I contributed quite a bit to Canada's victory in Oslo. I took great pride in winning that gold medal and in beating the Soviet team. I decided I should go out on top."

What a dream of a year he'd had, and then he simply turned his back on it and got on with the rest of his life! It seems impossible to imagine in our time of salary caps, and multi-million dollar contracts, and families sacrificing *all* in the hope of one child becoming a professional athlete. I've often wondered what it must have been like to live that kind of dream as a young man, and yet to have had the wisdom and perspective of my great uncle Connie.

I am reminded of the teaching of Rabbi Heschel who, in his book *The Sabbath*, observes that the world is at least as much about time as it is about space. We tend, however, to be drawn by the attractions of space – the realm of things, and of having – and not so much to the challenges of time, of being. "We must not forget that it is not a thing that lends significance to a moment; it is the moment that lends significance to things. The goal is not to have but to be, not to own but to give, not to control but to share, not to subdue but to be in accord."[2]

So what would your dream year be like? Would it be more about having or being? And when it was time to move on again, would you be able to leave the dream behind?

[1] Szymon Szemberg, "Broden's Feat Will See No Repeat," *International Ice Hockey Federation News*, Vol. 6, No. 2 (April 2002).

[2] Abraham Joshua Heschel, *The Sabbath* (New York: Farrar, Straus and Giroux, 1951).

23 Tea

Opinion polls throughout the world have consistently named two people as the most widely admired political leaders of the past generation. Each born in a remote village, they were originally named Lhamo Dhondrub and Rolihlahla by their parents. As they matured and began to take up their respective life's work, they later became known within their communities as Tenzin Gyatso and Dalibunga. They have entered history, of course, as the Dalai Lama and Nelson Mandela.

Neither of these political leaders is especially remembered for any ability they may have had to reduce taxes or to operate an efficient administrative system, or for the quality of their political analysis or strategic vision. It is not even on account of their major historical achievements, substantial though they have been, and celebrated with Nobel Prizes for Peace in 1989 and 1993: specifically, the over-turning of the system of apartheid, the preservation and renewal of Tibetan Buddhism, and the galvanizing of international support for the liberation of their oppressed and impoverished peoples.

Rather, people cite the personal attributes of the two men, their clarity of vision and their integrity of character in the face of adversity, as the basis of their significance. In the case of Nelson Mandela, it is his determination, commitment to principle, and utter dedication to justice, despite decades of imprisonment, persecution, and abuse, that people admire. In the case of the Dalai Lama, it is his ability to maintain a sense of patience and kindness, a spirit of compassion, and an attitude of openness and dialogue in relation to his enemies, despite spending virtually his entire life in exile from his homeland, and despite being constantly subject to the contempt of the forces that occupy it.

Both leaders stand as pre-eminent icons of our age because of their ability to bear witness to the possibility of a new future for humanity, which they do by expressing so fully their own human dignity. In particular, each of these leaders averted open conflict in their societies – and, in the case of Mandela's South Africa, an almost certain civil war – by their personal example of embracing the spirit of forgiveness and reconciliation.

Amnesty International was awarded the Nobel Peace Prize in 1977. For about five years during the 1990s, one of my special responsibilities as Deputy Secretary General was to coordinate relations with the other Laureates. Each year a number of them, at least those of like mind, would meet to discuss issues of common concern and sometimes to undertake joint initiatives. The person who always impressed me most on these occasions was the Dalai Lama, not simply because of his depth of wisdom, but especially because of his simple and unassuming humanity, often expressed in an infectious sense of humour and a mischievous spirit of playfulness.

One of my most enjoyable experiences with the Dalai Lama occurred during a long and very tiresome day I spent with him in Strasbourg recording a television program for ARTE, the joint European public network. The format of the program was demanding but straightforward enough – a three-hour series of interviews and panel discussions – but the conversations were constantly interrupted by misunderstandings and disagreements among the technicians. Mostly French and Germans, they seemed to be bickering over who was in control.

After several hours of this, and as the day began to stretch past mid-afternoon, the Dalai Lama leaned over to me and whispered, "You know, they all seem to be so preoccupied with their arguments that if we were to leave it would probably be a long time before they even notice. Let's see!" And with that we quietly slipped out of the studio, grabbed a taxi, and spent a happy hour doing a quick tour of the sites of Strasbourg. Of course, the studio was in a state of panic and pandemonium when we returned, but soon the recording resumed and this time the program was completed without further "technical difficulties."

But I suspect that my most memorable encounter with the Dalai Lama will always be the first time I met him. It was in 1993. I had heard that he would soon be passing through London, so I sent a message inviting him to stop by my office for tea. To my complete astonishment – and shock – he not

The Dalai Lama
Comes to Tea

only replied, but accepted! I can't remember what kind of tea we served, but I think he just had a glass of water. I showed him the files we held on him, and he took great interest in going through them, stopping now and again to smile or to point out some interesting detail to one of his assistants.

I asked him if he would be willing to address the Amnesty staff. He agreed without hesitation and word quickly spread around the office. Within a few moments, a couple of hundred of my colleagues gathered in the lunch room. After a few of his trademark jokes, the Dalai Lama grew solemn. Silence fell upon the room as he slowly, silently looked around. He seemed to make eye contact with each person present.

He then smiled and spoke carefully through his interpreter, anxious to ensure that his comments were conveyed
precisely: "I wanted to thank you for what you are doing,
but now I think that is not really appropriate. I am a simple
monk, and what I really want to say is simply that I believe
that the work all of you are doing – caring for the dignity
of strangers, protecting their rights – I believe this work is
sacred. I believe it is more important than prayer."

And with that he bowed, and left. I think many of the
people in the lunchroom that day felt changed in some way.
For me, every morning as I begin my work I look at this
photo, which I call "The Dalai Lama Comes to Tea," and I
remind myself to try to approach whatever I have to do that
day as if it were a form of prayer – as if it might be even *more*
important than prayer.

24 Coffee

I am a devotee of full-contact gardening. My efforts to exca-
vate flower beds from the ancient creek bed around our house
in Naramata have earned me a nickname: "The Rock-weiler."
I am proud of the nickname and of my gardening, though
my sometimes-aching back is less impressed. Full-contact
gardeners are people who know that the cheapest way to buy
Epsom salts is in 25 kilogram bags from the garden centre.

The hillside behind our new house in Penticton stretches
up to Redlands at an angle that is a little better than 45
degrees. Okay, it's closer to 60 degrees. To a committed full-
contact gardener, however, that can mean only one thing
– it's time for terracing!

Like many gardeners, digging in the earth is for me an
exercise in personal archaeology – an opportunity to reflect.
As I began to build my first terrace recently, I realized that I
was following a pattern that was already set in my mind, a
knowledge drawn from something I'd observed many years
ago. I remembered that, in fact, I began my international

human rights work almost exactly 25 years ago – in the magnificent rice terraces of Sagada, on the island of Luzon in the northern Philippines.

The extraordinary terraces of Sagada are a marvel of effort and engineering, and have sustained countless generations of the indigenous Kalinga and Bontoc tribal peoples, who continue to occupy the region. Today, the terraces are recognized as a United Nations World Heritage Site, but in the early 1980s they were slated to be flooded, and the people forcibly relocated, as part of Ferdinand Marcos' plan to develop the region. Ostensibly, the purpose of the dams was to generate electricity to serve the long-term needs and industrialization of the country. But in the eyes of many, Marcos' more immediate goal was to attend to the interests of an array of multi-national corporations, as well as to the insatiable greed of his own dictatorship – what came to be known as the "cleptocracy," a regime based on an addiction to theft.

I was sent to research the impact of the proposed mega-project on the local people, as some of the capital investment and technical assistance would be coming from Canada. The country was in the grip of an undeclared but nonetheless severe civil war. About a third of the country was controlled by the communist insurgents, largely as a result of poor people desperately resisting Marcos' attempts to push them off their traditional lands. That was precisely what had happened in this region, and I had been invited to visit the home of Macli'ing Dulag, a legendary tribal leader who had called on his people to defend their traditional lands, and who had been assassinated by Marcos' troops a few months previously.

It took three days to travel the 200 kilometres or so from Manila to the tiny village of Bugnay, mainly because of repeated detours through the jungle to avoid the many military checkpoints along the roads. After Macli'ing's death, the insurgents had entered the area to support the tribal people, who to that point had been armed only with spears. The village had now become a rebel stronghold under siege. The only access was over a swinging footbridge suspended high above the Chico River canyon. We inched across it on our hands and knees, placing the deck planks ahead of us one at a time, and taking them up again and relaying them along the line as we moved forward.

The village clinging to the mountainside was, at that time, an anthropologist's dream, seemingly untouched by modernity except for the newly-arrived communist guerrillas. By custom, I was to be hosted by the eldest woman of the community. We climbed the steep path and found her standing outside her house, pounding beans in a mortar and pestle, and weeping. Inquiries were made to find out what was the matter. I understood only a single word before the interpreter spoke. "She says she is weeping because she is ashamed. She says you are her guest, and she has heard that you like to drink coffee. She says she is upset because she has only these native coffee beans to offer you; she says she is ashamed because has no 'Nescafe.'"

I remember being stunned that the power of corporate advertising, as the arbiter of what is deemed to be of value, was such that it could reach its insidious way even to this utterly remote and tradition-bound place. Then again, here

I was, a young Canadian investigating the innocent but potentially devastating impact of money and expertise from my country on these people. It was my first real experience of what came to be known a decade later as globalization.

I spent several days in the village interviewing the people, enjoying the fine local coffee, and helping out with repairs to the ancient terraces in preparation for the next planting season. Among the Kalinga and the Bontoc, as with many tribal peoples, the division of labour assigned responsibility for preparing the fields to the men, care for the crop to the women, and planting and harvest to all.

After several years of struggle, Marcos was successfully resisted and eventually overthrown, though at a great cost of life and limb. But the dam was never built. The Kalinga and Bontoc people continue to draw life and inspiration from their land, and the wondrous terraces bestowed on them by their ancestors will be preserved for the next generation.

And now I find myself using the knowledge they shared with me on the hillside behind my house on Creekside Road. Perhaps I'll treat it as my own little tribute to them, a reminder of the ingenuity and determination required, if we are to survive and find a sustainable path to the future.

25 Storm

At the moment I am doing some work for the United Nations. Earlier this fall, I was asked to take on a fairly major piece of research and negotiation, as part of the UN reform program. So this month I am sampling the Christmas season in 11 different countries.

The issues I am working on – how to reorganize the UN system so that it can more quickly and effectively implement the Convention on the Rights of the Child – are at once fantastically simple and frustratingly complex. Simple because the real-life needs of the world's children are practical, evident, and urgent; complex because the solutions involve billions of dollars, thousands of staff, and the competing interests of dozens of governments.

Tonight I am in Rome, and unable to sleep because my mind is racing around the realities of the simple part, and is preoccupied with how to deal with the complex part. The rain is beating heavily on the cobblestones outside my hotel, ironically named Hotel Canada, near the Termini station. All of the hotel stationary, towels, and other accoutrements, are embossed with the Canadian coat of arms, and appear disconcertingly official. Beyond the Latin motto scrolled at the bottom of the seal, *"a mari usque ad mare,"* the connection between my homeland and the hotel – a 1930s classic, with terracotta tiles, marbled facades, shuttered windows, frescoed ceilings, and a caged, single-passenger "lift" – remains a complete mystery to me.

The storm outside is intense, and seems to be growing by the minute. Earlier in the evening, in fact, my plane had been struck by lightning on its final approach into Leonardo da Vinci airport. There was a loud bang from the left wing, the plane rocked and a bright flash filled the cabin for a moment. I am sure this happens regularly, but still I was surprised that none of my fellow passengers seemed to react or to even take any notice whatsoever. Travellers carried on their casual conversations without interruption, and businessmen impatiently continued to turn the pages of their newspapers, without so much as a sideways glance.

Puzzled, I turned to the man seated next to me and asked, "Didn't anyone see what just happened?" He looked around the cabin, gathered himself into the universal posture of nonchalance, shrugged, and waved away my concern. "Yes, I saw the flash and there was the noise, but I don't think the bolt actually hit the plane. Perhaps it was just nearby – very close maybe. Why pay it any notice?"

In the hotel, sleep apparently futile at the moment, I open the shutters and pull up a chair to sit and watch the rain in the night. Another bolt of lightning has just struck "very close" to the hotel. The thunder follows almost immediately and is deafening, shaking the building – and evidently the whole neighbourhood, because hundreds of car alarms have suddenly gone off. In response, the streets have filled with young people, singing and dancing in the rain. It reminds me of the dawn chorus in a tropical rainforest, where for a few moments it seems like the shouts, and cries, and songs of millions of birds fill the whole universe.

Surely no one could have slept through such a dramatic storm, but at breakfast I discover that many of my fellow travellers have slumbered comfortably through the night behind their closed shutters. It is time to get on with our simple and complex work, and I find myself wondering if we will be able to rise to the challenge that confronts us. The survival of the UN is bound up in its ability to address urgently the critical threats to our survival as a species and as a planet – threats that appear to us most clearly in the needs of the world's children.

Will we persist in our passive and oblivious nonchalance, resting in the easy hope of the inevitability of dawn, deluding ourselves with the conceit that the dangers – even if dramatic, even if very close – can be dismissed or held at a distance for a little while longer? Or will we finally wake up to face the storm that has gathered around us in the night?

26 Box

Back in the olden times, in the days before televisions had remote controls, when something went wrong with a program the following message would appear on the screen: "Technical difficulties are temporary. Please stand by, and do not adjust your set."

Believe it or not, most people would simply obey this instruction, and wait patiently and faithfully for some unseen person in control of the station to fix things. Maybe that's one of the reasons that the television was sometimes referred to as "the idiot box." These days we are both less patient and less obedient – and we have remotes – all of which I think are good things!

Perhaps it is already an over-worn cliché, but as we enter this new year I am struck by the way we are continually urged to "think outside the box." Personally, I find it encouraging, because perhaps it means, at the very least, that we are recognizing that we are actually *in* a box. This, too, is a good thing, because as a species on this planet we have allowed ourselves to become trapped within a rigid and destructive box of our own making, and we urgently need to face up to a crisis not simply of well-being, but of basic survival. Lincoln put it well in his annual message of 1862: "The dogmas of the quiet past are inadequate to the stormy present. As our case is new, so we must think anew and act anew. We must disenthrall ourselves, and then we shall save our country."

I am hopeful that the call to "think outside the box" may represent much more than the simple recognition of a need. I believe it may also signal a shift in some of the essential attitudes and behaviours that we must address if anything is to change. It suggests that we are coming to understand that diverse perspectives on problems are valuable, that alternative explanations or solutions are possible, and that we actually have the ability to think new things and to learn together in new ways.

In fact, if you look, you can see it happening. Recently, I met someone whose job title is "Chief Knowledge Officer." With a desk on the 18th floor of a corporate glass tower in downtown Montreal, her task is to work with groups of people across the country to figure out what we need to know, and how we can best learn the skills we need, in order to overcome the absurd yet persistent scourge of poverty and exclusion in our society.

But my favourite job title of all is "Explorer in Residence." The National Geographic Society has appointed nine adventurous people to this position, to try to discover how we can best understand, protect, and live together on this planet. One of these people is from British Columbia – the ethno-botanist Wade Davis. One of the key insights emerging from their explorations is precisely this need to be open to diverse approaches to seeing and understanding.

One of their studies examined the records of the different responses of indigenous peoples in various parts of the world to their first encounter with Europeans. In the case of some aboriginal groups in Australia, it was found that the very notion of sailing ships was so completely outside the frame of reference of their lives, experience, and imaginations – their "box" – that they did not visually register the appearance of the ships on the horizon, or even the presence of the new strangers, until physically confronted by them on the beach. For many, that was too late. Apparently, contrary to our conventional thinking, it is not so much that we need to see in order to believe, but that we need first to believe, or at least to imagine, in order to see.

Other studies, also involving indigenous peoples and alternative faculties of intuitive understanding, are investigating the colours blue and green. Before the Spanish arrived, the Mayan language had distinct words for the many subtle varieties of blue. When the conquistadores wrote the first Mayan-Spanish dictionary, however, they referred to most of them simply as *azur*.

If the Mayan language becomes extinct, as is the prospect for some 2,400 of the world's 6,000 languages, we will have lost not only the words for these different colours, but also the very ability to see them. I know from my own experience that after I've spent a few days in a situation where

I'm living and working in French, I begin to dream in French – and that there are dreams and feelings that I can *only* have in French. Professional interpreters tell me they have exactly the same experience in their various languages. One scholar has described the situation almost poetically:

> There are nine different words in Maya for the co-
> lour blue in the comprehensive Porrua Maya-Span-
> ish Dictionary, but just three Spanish translations,
> leaving six butterflies that can be seen only by the
> Maya, proving beyond doubt that when a language
> dies six butterflies disappear from the consciousness
> of the earth.[1]

It seems that each culture or language or spiritual tradition, no matter how remote or marginal, offers a unique perspective on the world that bears some unique facet of truth or reality – and potentially some part of the solution to our increasingly shared problems.

One of the explorations Wade Davis is involved in deals with precisely this issue. Originally intending to study the medicinal plants used by a tribal group in the Amazon, researchers became aware that they were unable to locate some of the plants that were supposedly widely available in the tropical rainforest. They have concluded that they are completely unable to see, at least in the jungle setting, some of the shades of green that the indigenous people refer to, and are easily able to distinguish and to perceive.

The cure for some of the world's most terrible diseases may be right in front of the researchers. But staring longer into the jungle doesn't seem to help them develop the ability to distinguish between the forest and the trees. Trying *different*, rather than simply trying *harder*, seems to be the key. Sharing deeply in other peoples' lives, listening to different cultures and experiences with care and respect, and being open to trying different approaches and perspectives – these seem to be first steps in learning to look "outside the box."

---

1   Earl Shorris, "The Last Word," *Harper's*, August 2000.

27 Mappery

One of the many words that Shakespeare coined is "mappery." It occurs in *Troilus and Cressida*, and refers to a condition that another writer has described as being "an ecstatic contemplator of things cartographic." I have a serious case of this affliction.

The fact is, I read maps. I mean it's something I do just for the pleasure of it. I read maps the way some people eagerly study the latest styles in a fashion magazine, or settle down for an intimate evening with a new thriller from a favourite author. On most mornings, I spend half an hour or so before breakfast poring over an unfolded map. I've done this all my life.

I suppose it is somewhat strange, but one of the benefits is that I rarely get lost. No matter where I am in the world, I somehow seem to be able to recognize the place – I can usually look out of an airplane window over Central Africa or Southeast Asia and know what town or river is silently slipping by far below.

I study all kinds of maps – straightforward geographical maps; fanciful historical maps, filled with mystery and conjecture; ordinance surveys, with topographical contours and every building or hedgerow carefully plotted. I even study more analytical maps, such as those that show language distribution or population density. My current favourite is a set of maps tracing the expansion of tartan weaving technology, and the spread of Celtic languages in Central Asia 4000 years ago.

Sometimes my morning mappery is just mindfully aimless wandering, but often I have a particular question in mind. A couple of months ago, I opened the atlas intending to figure out, solely on the basis of geographical considerations, what would be the ideal place in the world to live. Taking into account latitude, elevation, access to water, and other such factors, I selected a place in Mexico called Lago de Chapala. I knew nothing about the place, but it looked exotic and I became increasingly enchanted with it as my imagination began to play.

At breakfast, I announced my discovery. A friend, who happened to be visiting, screwed up her nose with knowing familiarity and said, "Oh, yeah, I spent a year there once. You never heard of it? I think D. H. Lawrence lived there in the 1920s, when he was depressed. Very pretty, but I hated the place. The guy I was living with turned out to be a creep, and the whole lake is surrounded by expensive condos owned by rich Canadians."

My fantasy suddenly in jeopardy, I did a quick Google search and was dismayed to find that there are indeed so many Canadian retirees living at Lago de Chapala that they even have their own newsletter. (Sadly, the newsletter seems to be mainly preoccupied with rising taxes and rampant pollution, much as if the people who wrote it had simply stayed home.) In fact, so many highly consumptive Canadians crowd this particular patch of paradise that the lake is rapidly shrinking, and the Mexican government has declared it biologically exhausted and unsustainable. I guess when it comes to perfect places, the reality on the ground is not always as it appears on a map or as in one's imagination.

Another one of my recent searches sought to identify the world's most isolated place. This time I chose a place that doesn't appear on many maps, either because its location is so awkward – it tends to fall just off the edge of the page, or deep into the crease of most atlases – or because it has simply been forgotten. Clipperton Island is a coral atoll in the Pacific Ocean. Technically part of French Polynesia, it is so far east that its nearest neighbours live in Guatemala. No one actually lives on Clipperton, but my curiosity was piqued by the fact that is it known to the French as "Ile de la Passion" – the island of passion, or of suffering, depending on one's interpretation.

Pirates used Clipperton Island for centuries because it offered an ideal place to hide out and, according to legend, to hide treasure. Eventually the island came to be valued for its deposits of guano, the fertilizer formed from thousands of years of bird droppings. In 1906, a British mining company established a settlement and built a lighthouse. A ship would arrive every two months to bring supplies to the more than

100 men, women, and children on the island, and to carry away the guano. However, wars arose in distant places: first the Civil War in Mexico, and then the First World War in Europe. Regular shipments to Clipperton Island were interrupted and before long, as staff changed and as institutional memory was lost, the visits ceased altogether.

What happened next remains something of a mystery, pieced together from the shame and silence of those who really knew. It seems that, one by one, the men of the settlement vanished, until only one was left – a brute named Victoriano Alvarez, who occupied the lighthouse and who promptly proclaimed himself king. A reign of terror ensued as he preyed upon the women and the children of the community.

Eventually, the women banded together, devised a trap, and managed to kill the "king." In 1917, an American gunship, the USS Yorkton, finally happened upon the island and picked up the last survivors – four women and six children. It has been uninhabited ever since, although some say it was used to test secret weapons during World War II.

Isolated perhaps, and certainly forgotten, even Clipperton Island could not distance itself from the deepest currents and conflicts of human experience. It seems that the limits and boundaries of our finest maps are not able to contain the tragic forces of history.

Today, I am in Tokyo. I took the morning off from my negotiating work to visit a temple in the Shinagawa district, which is famous for its dry-land meditation garden. The hotel staff kindly prepared a detailed map for me, and I spent a couple of happy hours searching for the Tozen-ji in this highly ordered and impossibly chaotic agglomeration of 32 million people. I went up streets, down back lanes, through tunnels, and even followed an overgrown pathway through a creaking old bamboo grove. But I never found the temple or its garden.

I'm sure the map was wrong. Of course, I suppose I could have asked someone for directions, but one of the symptoms of those who suffer from severe mappery – especially the men – is that they tend to have a certain reluctance about that sort of thing. At least when exploring! Some even believe that it is because we actually enjoy being lost – it's the only way we ever manage to find ourselves.

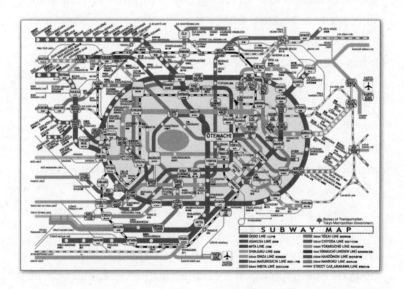

28 Burning

In most cultures and religions, fire is a symbol of purification. It represents the cleansing that results from efforts to overcome the addictions, temptations, and weaknesses that prevent us from living to our full potential, as individuals and as communities.

This kind of transformation often involves spiritual practices or other disciplines that are arduous or that involve some kind of difficult struggle in order to achieve the strength or wisdom required to face a challenge. The notions of "baptism by fire" in the West, or the funeral pyre in the East, reflect this image of transformation. Political prisoners in the Philippines once gave me an inscribed plaque they had made. It read, "Those who would give light must endure burning."

The trouble is, it has traditionally been far more attractive, especially as a political option, to look *outside* rather than *inside* for the source of our troubles or failures; to turn on others as objects of an evil we prefer to imagine as being alien to ourselves. "Purification" is seen less as a personal discipline and improvement and more as a motive for attacking and destroying others. After a couple of decades of ethnic cleansing throughout the world, I find myself fearful of any rituals that involve burning.

Almost inevitably, burning rituals tend to be conducted as a service to the ideological mind – that approach to the world that has given us a century of the most extreme forms of violence and mass suffering, and that seems to be spreading again. The ideological perspective proceeds from the idea that there is only one proper or acceptable way to live, only one proper or acceptable set of beliefs, only one appropriate form of organization. It imagines the world fundamentally in terms of "us" and "them," and is most succinctly and fearfully captured in the ancient phrase that resurfaced in a somewhat twisted manner in November 2001: "If you are not for us, you are against us."

For many, our image of ritual burning is the huge bonfire held by the Nazis to signal their rise to absolute power in the spring of 1933, when about 20,000 "degenerate" books were burned in Berlin. The Nazis burned books not because they objected to quantum physics or certain economic theories, but because they wanted to make it clear that their vision of the world had no place for authors like Einstein, who were Jews, or for others who were Communists.

This practice of burning books is not particular to the Nazis, or even to modern times. Records from ancient China reveal that, in 213 BCE, the emperor ordered all copies of the first book by Confucius to be burned. From at least 1239 CE, one pope after another called for the burning of Jewish and other "heretical" books. Indeed, book burning often accompanied the burning of the heretics themselves, sometimes as fuel, underlining the fact that such acts are neither expressions of protest nor objection to ideas, but an assault by ideologues on the very notion that differences may be tolerated.

It is tempting to think that such attitudes and behaviours belong to distant times and faraway places, but it is worth remembering that public burnings of heretics under the "authority" of the Spanish Inquisition continued in North America until 1850. Indeed, the Inquisition's successor institution in the Vatican continued to enforce an "Index of Proscribed Books" until 1966. I am not that old (really!), but I grew up in a cosmopolitan Canadian city of more than two million people in which, when I was a boy, only one bookstore dared to sell books on the Vatican's Index. The shop was regularly vandalized and was the target of arsonists; the owner was periodically threatened and assaulted. A simple man of great courage, Henri Tranquille (also known as "Monsieur Livre") died in November 2005, in Montreal.

Book burners believe that not only certain *ideas* should be purged from society, but also, inevitably, that those who hold the ideas, and ultimately diversity itself, must be eradicated as well. Book-burning is a characteristic of genocide; it is no accident that one of the precursors to the Bosnian war was the burning of the National Library by Serb forces in 1992. Historians believe it was probably the largest single incident of book-burning in modern history.

This is more than a theoretical concern for me because, in fact, I've had the peculiar experience of having one of my own books publicly burned. In 1995, I co-authored a book on human rights in Sudan called *The Tears of Orphans*. Among other things, it criticized aspects of Sudan's Criminal Code, which prescribed punishments such as flogging and amputation; practices which are considered "torture or cruel, inhuman or degrading treatment" under international law. We urged the government to consider alternative interpretations of Islamic law that would prohibit such practices, as had already been done in many Muslim countries. I had proposed to the government that we hold meetings in Khartoum to discuss our concerns and possible reforms.

The government put out a public statement agreeing to the visit, and invited me to come to Geneva first to discuss arrangements. There, in the elegant embassy, I sat down with the Minister of Justice, who promptly informed me that the government had determined that I was "an enemy of Islam" for suggesting any deviation from their interpretation of Shari'ah law, and that a public burning of my book was scheduled to take place in Khartoum the next day.

His statement was intended partly as a threat, and partly as a kindness; the minister was advising that if I came to Khartoum they would have to treat me accordingly! The visit did not proceed, and the hope of any constructive dialogue – along with the opportunity to improve the living conditions of countless people destined to face yet another decade of abuse and war – went up in smoke.

There have been a lot of ritual burnings during the past couple of years – of cars in France; of Danish flags; and of books, sacred and otherwise. Without in any way minimizing the legitimate feelings of offence experienced by many Muslims, it is certainly also the case that the violent responses to the Danish cartoons of Muhammad were contrived and manipulated by ideologues, by those opposed to difference and intent on defeating dialogue. At the same time, I am alarmed at how readily many in our society would sacrifice freedom of expression in the name of some supposed multicultural tolerance and respect, or perhaps simply out of a vain yearning for peace and quiet.

The deeper we step into the 21st century, the clearer it becomes that we must take seriously the reality and the significance of the world's great spiritual traditions. We urgently need to discover creative ways of relating with each other, in open, honest, and respectful relationships. Yet we seem increasingly caught in a complex dialectic of distrust and resentment that allows little room for dialogue, and that threatens to condemn us to a perpetual spiral of division and conflict. A headline in *The Economist* captured not only the difficulties of the current moment, but the dynamic that has characterized much of the 1,300-year relationship between the Islamic world and the Christian and humanist traditions of the West: "Mutual Incomprehension, Mutual Outrage."[1]

Although they may not legitimately reflect the beliefs or behaviours of most people in their communities, extremists or fundamentalists have come to assume a pre-eminent role as leaders or representatives for many of the world religions during the past decade, at least in the eyes of the media and of popular culture. These extremist forces tend to oppose dialogue and to erect obstacles to understanding. Too often, they have combined with virulent nationalist or other ideological sentiments, resulting in repression and violence. We cannot escape our history. Our only options are to blindly repeat it, or to create a new future by trying to understand, and to build healthy relationships with, those with whom we share this planet.

I believe that freedom of expression and the ability to engage in genuine dialogue are, ultimately, the only defences we have against ideologues, and the tyranny, intolerance, and fear that are their constant companions. Upholding human rights can be challenging, and real dialogue can be tough. Dialogue is not about being nice, or about pretending that we are all the same. It requires that we honestly engage our real differences; that we relate to each other constructively, even when we are in opposition; and that we stand in solidarity with each other when one of us is attacked.

Most of all, real dialogue requires that we recognize and be open to the fact that we both may be changed by our discourse. The defence of human rights demands that we commit to treating ourselves and each other with profound and passionate respect. The symbol for both interfaith dialogue and for the human rights movement is the candle – fire for giving light, not for burning.

---

[1] *The Economist*, 11 February 2006 (vol. 378, No. 8464).

29 Flight 000

One of the less dramatic but most significant consequences of the War on Terror is the creeping encroachment on some of our fundamental and supposedly cherished rights – the rights to freedom of expression and of thought. I say "supposedly cherished," because with each new restriction that is imposed, it becomes apparent that many people in our society actually place very little value on these rights and are ready to abandon them with little more than an indifferent shrug.

I'm speaking not only about the complex security laws hurriedly adopted in Washington and in Ottawa in the weeks following 9/11 – which allow people to be imprisoned indefinitely without charge or evidence – though certainly those laws should worry us all. And I'm speaking not only about the secret, paranoid conspiracies of our public security agencies, which allow government officials to aid, abet, and acquiesce in the abduction and torture of Canadian citizens in Syrian prisons.

I'm thinking also about the many ways that a climate of fear and self-censorship has gathered around us, and has begun to infect many aspects of public life. One of the more recent and insidious examples is provided by Indigo Books. The largest bookseller in Canada, Indigo Books decided to ban an issue of *Harper's Magazine* because it featured an article discussing the Danish cartoons of Muhammad.

Echoing the feeble justifications of the CBC, *The Globe and Mail*, and numerous other members of the "free" press, an internal corporate memo sent to all Indigo stores – as well as its Coles and Chapters branches – explained that the article may offend some Muslims. It went on to note that the cartoons have "been known to ignite demonstrations around the world," making it clear that Indigo's real motivation for pulling the magazine was fear. The feeling of fear is understandable enough, in my view. It's just too bad it can't be openly acknowledged and honestly addressed.

It is important to mention that the article in question, "Drawing Blood: Outrageous Cartoons and the Art of Outrage," was written by the most prominent political cartoon journalist in America, and that it presents a scholarly discussion of the role of editorial cartooning during the past 200 years. As a subscriber to *Harper's*, I had read the article before the ban was put in place, and had recommended it to a number of people as the most insightful analysis of the cartoon controversy I'd yet seen.

Sadly, such scholarly reflection and critical thought is now deemed to be too offensive – or dangerous – to be permissible. I'm not sure what should be considered the greater scandal: the blatant hypocrisy and cynicism of Indigo Books, or the fact that their suppression of the magazine generated so little public concern. Try to imagine what any bookstore or library would look like if we removed all materials that might be offensive to some individual or group. The shelves would be empty, and a dark silence would soon gather around us. Having shunned the honest effort required for dialogue or for understanding, we would soon become prisoners of our own fears and prejudices, unable even to imagine alternatives, and become prone to acting aggressively to perceived threats.

Perhaps most Canadians have little sense of what is at stake if we abdicate our fundamental freedoms, even just a bit in the interests of good taste or of a quiet life. The most extreme example, I suppose, is North Korea. North Korea is usually described as "totalitarian," "paranoid," and "Stalinist," and even as part of the "axis of evil." It regularly threatens its neighbours with missiles and nuclear tests.

I've been to North Korea twice, once on an assignment for the World Council of Churches, and once as a special guest of the Inter-Parliamentary Union. Whatever words may be used to describe it, North Korea is fundamentally about complete control. I think the most chilling image I have of this comes from a visit I made to a kindergarten in Pyongyang, the capital city. The four-year-olds sat ramrod straight and silent at tables until the teacher gave the command "Be happy!" The children immediately erupted in cheers and laughter and clapping, and just as abruptly returned to their seats, silent and staring, when the teacher declared, "Enough happy!"

KIM IL SUNG

President of the Democratic People's Republic of Korea requests the pleasure of your company at a banquet in honour of the participants in the 85th Inter-Parliamentary Conference

on 29 April, 1991   at 19.00 hrs.
at Kumsusan Assembly Hall

You get a sense of how repressed and bizarre the political life of the country is long before you get there. Most visitors enter the country on a connecting flight through China – only you don't receive a ticket or a boarding card, you just get a letter of invitation from whatever organization is your "host." The letter tells you to go to the check-in hall at Beijing's international airport, and to wait.

Curious but obedient, I did as directed. However, I've never been very good at waiting, so eventually I began to ask at the different airline counters where to find the flight to Pyongyang. The staff simply pointed vaguely toward the middle of the vast hall. Feeling absurd, I nevertheless followed their instructions and gradually became aware of a couple dozen other travellers who seemed to be aimlessly standing around, or endlessly searching the monitors as if for some secret clue. We began stealing glances at each other, with a strange combination of recognition and suspicion. Finally, a man in a nondescript airline uniform walked to the middle of the room carrying a little sign that read, "Flight 000, Destination X." Without a word, all the lost strangers formed a line, and we dutifully followed the man through an unmarked exit and onto a North Korean plane.

The hotel in Pyongyang was modern and well-appointed, but came with some unusual services. There was a television in the room, but like all TVs and radios in North Korea it had only one switch – on/off. For the first five days of my first visit, the evening "news" broadcast consisted mainly of reports of what my colleagues and I had done that day. It was a great relief – probably for everyone in the country – when the President of the Seychelles arrived on a state visit and became the new focus of obsessive media attention. Otherwise, TV consisted of endless lectures denouncing the country's many enemies, and providing detailed instructions on the correct line of thought – that of the "Great Leader"; or of his son, the "Dear Leader" and current President, pictures of whom peered down on every room in every building.

My hotel room was not only cleaned every day while I was out, it was also thoroughly searched. In fact, only every second room was occupied by a guest; the intervening rooms were reserved for those who monitored us 24 hours a day. One morning, the guests on my floor decided to test the surveillance. At exactly 7 a.m., each of us turned on our showers and then shouted, "Damn, no towels!" We then opened our doors and looked out into the corridor. Within seconds, it was filled with men in suits running from the other rooms carrying stacks of fresh towels, rushing about and bumping into each other.

I have been detained twice by the police in North Korea, once for jogging and once for riding the subway. The jogging incident was just a misunderstanding; I suppose any individual running in North Korea is assumed to be trying to escape from something, and the police simply acted instinctively. The subway was a more serious incident, in that there was a real danger I might have had unsupervised contact with ordinary people – precisely my objective.

With some diversions from my colleagues, I had managed to leave the hotel after dark, and made my way to the nearest subway station. However, I soon discovered that there are four different types of money in North Korea (for the political elite, for foreign dignitaries, for proletarians or ordinary workers, and for "sub-proletarians" – whoever they are!). The money *I* had could not be used to buy a subway ticket (a proletarian activity). I decided to try something that had probably never been seen in North Korea, before or since. I stood outside the station as endless lines of workers streamed past, bowed my head, and raised my hands in the universal posture of a beggar. Immediately a crowd surrounded me, and, without a word of discussion, the workers filled my cupped hands with proletarian notes, more than enough to get on the subway. I got about four stations down the line before the alarm was raised and the police boarded the train and took me away.

Throughout my second visit to North Korea, with the Inter-Parliamentary Union, I pressed the authorities for a copy of the Criminal Code. The formal reason I gave for wanting the text was so that I could carry out an assessment of it in relation to international human rights standards. But really, I just wanted to find out if it actually existed, as no one outside the country had seen the North Korean basic law. Every day, I asked for a copy, or suggested adjustments to our itinerary to stop at a bookstore or at a court building. But there was invariably some excuse that made it impossible – the store is closed due to holidays, the building is under renovations, and so on.

Finally, on the last day, after a particularly long meeting, my "host" suggested that we take a break and visit the "Great Study Hall of the People," the national library. We climbed the stone steps of the enormous stolid building, and took the elevator to the seventh floor. This, he said, was the section on law and politics, as we walked through the gloom past rank upon rank of barren shelves and vacant desks. He ushered me down a particular aisle and stopped in front of a single steel shelf on which were four thin green volumes. He took one down and gave it to me – a copy of the Criminal Code of North Korea. Embossed in gold and in mint condition, the text was in English and inscribed as a gift to me.

I was touched by the near intimacy of the gesture, but also troubled by the thought that this basic legal text may actually have been created or contrived during the past week simply to satisfy my demands and to try to ensure a favourable report to the parliamentarians. Most of all, though, I was disturbed by all of the empty shelves that surrounded us – a whole library without books, the ultimate expression of a regime that could not tolerate the challenge of diversity, the risk of dialogue, or the right to freedom of thought.

It is an extreme image, I know, but one that I wish the executives of Indigo Books, and others who act in fear of the open and respectful exchange of ideas, might hold in their hearts. It will certainly be the image I have in mind the next time I am tempted to shop at Coles or Chapters, or hear about a magazine being banned.

30 Statue

A couple of weeks ago, I was teaching a course at the Naramata Centre. After a session, I walked out to the parking lot
with one of the participants and noticed a sticker on his car
– one of those twisted ribbons with the slogan, "I support our
troops." You see a lot of those stickers in the United States,
and they seem to have begun appearing in Canada since we
entered the war in Afghanistan in a big way.

I've always been puzzled by the slogan. I mean, who
doesn't "support our troops"? After all, like it or not, everyone who pays taxes in this country supports our troops in
the most direct and concrete way possible. And I am sure that
most Canadians support the members of our armed forces
through our spirit of concern and our hope that they will not
come to any harm. So, when I see a vague slogan like that,
I have the uneasy suspicion that I'm being presented with
a piece of political propaganda, something fundamentally
manipulative and dishonest.

I asked my friend why he had it on his car. After churning it over for a while, he agreed that the real purpose of the sticker was probably to encourage people to support our new military role in Afghanistan (or in Iraq, if you're American). It had nothing to do with the troops, and everything to do with the political decisions about how the troops are being used. In a sense, it's the inverse of the "human shield" tactic. Instead of soldiers hiding behind civilians to prevent the other side from shooting back, some of our political leaders are trying to hide behind the troops to prevent citizens from questioning or criticizing their decision to go to war.

It would seem that they think it better that we not think or talk too much about the war. At the beginning of the current military deployment, the prime minister sought to avoid a parliamentary debate, and even instructed officials to downplay or to try to avoid memorials or other events that would draw public attention to deaths and injuries among Canadian troops. Those politicians are right to be concerned, because most people in our country are either confused about or uncomfortable with our involvement in Afghanistan. Canadians are confused because there seems to be no clear purpose and compelling rationale for the war. And they are uncomfortable because the role we are playing is so profoundly out of keeping with our traditional commitment as peacekeepers in the world.

Last week, I contacted a dozen people across the country and asked them what they understood the purpose of the war to be. Most said they simply didn't know. Some said they thought it was to placate U.S. criticism of Canada, or to allow the Americans to better concentrate on Iraq. A couple of people referred vaguely to the "war on terror." Not one person said it was to protect Canadians, or even Afghan civilians for that matter.

Okay, maybe my friends and family are just particularly ill-informed, but I doubt it. In any case, if our leaders really want us to support this war they will need to come out from behind the slogans and offer us some meaningful explanations. Of course, it may be that they simply do not care about whether we support the war or not.

I suspect that many Canadians may tacitly accept our involvement in the war in Afghanistan, because they continue to imagine it as an expression of our role as international peacekeepers. We rightly honour heroes such as Romeo Dallaire and other courageous and dedicated representatives of this tradition, but it is time we recognize that this cherished identity is largely drawn and borrowed from an increasingly distant past.

When the Nobel Prize for peace was awarded to the UN Peacekeepers in 1988, we Canadians presumed to claim it as "ours." And fair enough. Lester Pearson basically invented the system in 1956, and Canada had participated in almost all of the operations since then, more than any other country to that point. We put up a nice statue in Ottawa, and issued a new ten dollar bill to commemorate our peacekeepers.

Since 1988, it has been a very different story, as our participation in UN peacekeeping has gradually declined, almost to the point of non-existence. It is a difficult truth to confront, but Canada is now at best a marginal player, and

no longer ranks even among the top 50 of the 78 countries
that contribute to UN peacekeeping operations. Of the 69,146
troops currently deployed in 15 UN peacekeeping operations
around the world, as of the end of 2006, a grand total of
15 are Canadian. If police and observers are included, the
number of Canadians assigned to UN peacekeeping operations rises to 132. But in terms of actual troops, we have one
person in Cyprus, three in the Golan Heights, four in Haiti,
and seven in Sudan.

By contrast, Bangladesh currently has 9,681 troops serving as peacekeepers in various countries, and Pakistan has
some 9,867. Canada is not alone in its withdrawal from or
outsourcing of peacekeeping duties. Eight countries – Bangladesh, Ethiopia, Ghana, India, Jordan, Nepal, Pakistan, and
Uruguay – each contribute more UN troops than all 26 NATO
countries combined.

When I was doing some human rights work last year
in the war-ravaged area along the Burundi-Congo border,
people would wave from their houses and call out to me as I
passed by, "Hey, Pakistani, bienvenue! Welcome!" If you are
a refugee fleeing a war in Africa and desperately looking for
protection, your image of a UN peacekeeper is likely to be of
someone from South Asia, probably a Muslim, and almost
certainly not of a Canadian.

Also by contrast, since 9/11, Canada has spent more than
$4 billion on military operations in Afghanistan – a figure
that is ballooning by the day now that we have some 2,300
troops there. During the same time, we spent less than $215
million on the UN peacekeeping system. I'm glad the Paki-

stanis and others have picked up the slack. But I'm not at all comfortable that, as a nation, we seem to have abandoned our dedication to international peacekeeping.

I have not included our participation in the International Security Assistance Force in Afghanistan in this discussion. Whatever one's view of that mission may be, we must be clear about what it is and what it is not. It is *not* a UN peacekeeping mission; it is a NATO military operation comprising, as they put it, a "coalition of the willing." Of course, there are development and humanitarian aspects to the mission. But it is fundamentally a military operation – a war conducted with the goal, repeatedly articulated in the most explicit terms, of "completely eradicating the enemy," identified either as terrorists or the Taliban, as if those were precisely definable groups.

In case you are wondering, my own view is simply shaped by history and by context. An external military operation dedicated to eradicating a culturally or ethnically defined and cause-oriented group has always failed. Further, regardless of their intentions, any NATO force in this context must inevitably be perceived by many if not most people in Afghanistan as a military occupation of "Muslim lands" by "the West."

The Afghan mission may secure territory, and it may succeed in time in winning over the hearts and minds of some, and perhaps even most of the population. But it is not likely to create a durable peace, because it is guided by an assumption that the enemy, the forces of evil, can be objectified in an "other," and that they can and should be eradicated. Peace will never become a reality if we try to base it upon eradication of the enemy – however heinous we may consider them. Peace will only come when we base it on building a relationship between enemies, however tentative or limited that relationship may be.

This is the hard work of reconciliation. Reconciliation is not about enemies forgetting what happened or coming to like each other. It is about creating the conditions that will allow enemies to relate to each other on the basis of their authentic identities, instead of ones defined by their mutually perceived roles as victim or perpetrator. It is not about achieving our values and goals at all costs, nor is it about compromising with the values or interests of the other. It is about constructing a collaborative dialogue that may allow us both to discover an entirely new way to resolve our conflict.

When it comes to working for peace, we seem content to have a nice statue and some comforting memories about how principled we were. We can pretend, and indulge our well-developed sense of self-satisfaction. Perhaps we need to start having serious discussions about this war, and about what kind of international role we want to invest our money, our values, and our soldier's lives in. After all, we never needed manipulative slogans or borrowed bumper stickers to generate public support for our troops when we sent them into dangerous situations in Bosnia, the Golan Heights, or the more than 50 other peacekeeping operations we've been involved in since 1956.

It is time we did more than support our troops. It is time we also respected them – by ensuring they are not used as pawns for political agendas, and by ensuring that when we *do* send them abroad, it is to clearly and effectively uphold the most deeply-held values and purposes of our country.

31 Arafat

It has been another terrible month for people on all sides of the turmoil in the Middle East. Yet another horrific attack on a bus by suicide bombers has resulted in more retaliatory strikes on other communities. Whether in Lebanon or Israel, Gaza or the West Bank, hundreds more families have been left lost in grief, or struggling to deal with loved ones suddenly maimed and disabled. Perhaps the worst thing of all is that these words could have been written about almost any month in recent memory – and likely will continue to describe the situation for the foreseeable future.

Soon we will enter the season marking the anniversary of the establishment of Israel in 1948 – celebrated as "independence day" in Israel, and denounced as "the great catastrophe" among Palestinians. No doubt there will be another cycle of violence and suffering. Perhaps the greatest tragedy is that most people on all sides deeply yearn for peace, yet as members of their respective societies they are far from being able to move toward it.

The problem is not that it is so difficult to figure out what needs to be done to find a solution to the decades of conflict. Sure, it requires confronting some harsh truths and swallowing some bitter pills, but the fact is that almost all of those involved already fully recognize and accept the essential ingredients.

1. The Israelis and the Palestinians must accept each other's legitimate right to exist and prosper as independent nation states.

2. Both sides, and their supporters, must stop pointing blaming fingers at the other, and instead commit to taking full responsibility for their own actions.

3. Palestinian refugees must abandon their right to return to their ancestral homes in Israel, and the international community needs to support them in dealing with the dispossession and sense of injustice this will entail.

4. Israel must withdraw its settlements and forces from all the Syrian, Lebanese, and Palestinian territories it has occupied since 1967, and the international community needs to support them in overcoming the sense of insecurity this will entail.

5. All sides and parties must become committed and accountable to the Geneva Conventions and to international law.

Unfortunately, building peace is rarely simply a technical matter of knowing the right recipe or list of ingredients. It usually means dealing with whole peoples who have lived their entire lives in a context of war – a condition in which war has been their sole point of reference for what is real in life, and in which war has become, literally, "normal." Building peace is fundamentally about enabling people to find the confidence and the vision to engage in the hard work of constructing a new reality, a new concept of normal. It is about helping to foster the conditions that may give rise to trust and hope. It is difficult and long-term work, because it is not solely a challenge of global political forces – it is also a matter of deeply personal realities.

In Israel and in Palestine – and in Lebanon, and elsewhere – it will require engaging the almost unfathomable depths of resentment, grinding despair, and unending rage that naturally binds the hearts of so many people. It is tough work.

A few years ago, I had a glimpse of that harsh and bitter reality. I had been asked to chair local public hearings on human rights violations in northern Israel along the Lebanon border. Hundreds of people pressed into the meeting halls to give testimony to the indignities and atrocities suffered by their families and neighbours.

The grievances often extended back decades, but, unrecognized and unresolved, they persisted as a powerful presence in people's lives. From the outset, the witnesses screamed their testimony. Soon no one had any patience for awaiting their turn at the microphone, and countless people stood throughout the room at the same time, shouting of their suffering. It took me a while to realize that it was not anger directed at me, but just anger that needed to be expressed to someone in "authority," in a situation where it seems that no one ever listens with care to the experience of the "other."

I went on to Gaza to hold negotiations with Yasser Ara-
fat, then president of the Palestine Authority. It was our first
meeting, and I was taken aback to discover that this notorious adversary was such a frail old man. As our meeting wore
on through the night, I noticed he had to focus more and
more of his effort on controlling the tremors that betrayed
his struggle with a degenerative neurological disease. Out
of respect, I tried to maintain eye contact, but at one point I
looked down just as his hands began to shake.

When I looked up again, I saw that he had caught my
glance and for a few moments we shared a very uncomfortable silence. In the context of the Middle East conflict, it
seems that political leadership means never admitting one's
own weakness or failure – even to oneself. One of the key
challenges to be faced in building peace in the Middle East is

to take seriously the fact that it is real human beings – and not simply the one-dimensional ideological enemies we find so easy to construct – who are involved on all sides and at all levels. Perhaps the greatest cost of our current politics is our inability or unwillingness to acknowledge our personal realities, or to respond to our human limitations, in ourselves and in each other.

In the midst of the current tragedy and violence, I find glimmers of hope in a couple of developments. Of course, there continue to be many distortions and manipulations in the mutual accusations of the two sides, but there also seems to be a more balanced and more mature awareness emerging among the general public. This appears to be reflected in a recognition that

A. Israel has a legitimate right and need to act in self-defence, and indeed that Israel is under a real threat and attack.

B. Hamas and Hezbollah are official organizations operating with the support of other states in an international context, and need to be treated as such.

C. A unilateral ceasefire is not a reasonable expectation, and ensuring the protection of civilians on all sides is an international responsibility.

D. Hezbollah, in particular, acts militarily in a manner that manipulates civilians and intentionally places them at risk.

E. Israel needs to act militarily with due care for proportionality and civilian safety, and often has clearly failed to do so.

The thing I find most encouraging is that there appears to be a new willingness to see the impact of the conflict on ordinary people on both sides. I was at a family event in Montreal during the first few days of the recent war in Lebanon. This is the Jewish side of my family, and discussions are usually forcefully and narrowly framed in terms of support for Israel. But the attitude was very different this time, because of the family of Lebanese-Canadians killed on the first day of bombing.

I came down for breakfast and found everyone staring at the pictures on the front page of the *Gazette*. They were not images of tanks or devastated buildings – just family photos of neighbours from our home town of Ville St-Laurent, or Ville St-Liban, as the suburb is now known to some. My sister-in-law looked up with shock and said, "Oh my God, it's the man from the pharmacy on Cote-St-Luc Road!"

There was no less support for Israel, but at the same time there was no longer any easy distinction between "us" and "them," no longer a willingness to objectify, or to justify, or diminish, or disregard the suffering of the innocent people on the "other" side. I think our best hope rests in the discovery and embrace of such an expanded sense of inclusion, taking seriously that it is real human beings who are involved on all sides and at all levels of the conflict.

32 Ceasefire

A welcome ceasefire has settled uncomfortably on southern Lebanon. It is certainly welcome to the civilians living on either side of the border in that, given the option, it is always better not to feel in constant danger of being shot or bombed at any moment. It is also welcome to the Canadian and other Western governments, since it relieves them of some of the pointed political pressure of taking sides in the face of the demands of different trading partners and of competing constituencies at home.

At the same time, the ceasefire is uncomfortable, mainly for two reasons. First, because international peacekeeping has become highly unfashionable among those same Western governments. Most of them have expressed a deep reluctance to make any serious or potentially long-term commitment to peacekeeping in the region. Canada, for example, apparently remains willing to fight an ambiguous and unpopular war in Afghanistan until at least 2009, but has recently withdrawn its last UN peacekeepers from the Golan Heights. Second, the ceasefire is uncomfortable because neither the Israeli nor the Hezbollah leadership truly believes that the ceasefire is either necessary or desirable. This is reflected in the fact that both sides continue to "test" the ceasefire with occasional bombing raids or mortar attacks.

There are two harsh realities about the creation of a ceasefire. On the one hand, a ceasefire cannot be imposed from the outside unless the international community is committed to actively supporting it by being there – and for the long term, if necessary. That remains a highly uncertain prospect in Lebanon. On the other hand, although it would be pleasant to think that two sides agree to a ceasefire because of their concern for the suffering of civilians, the perhaps cynical but more accurate truth is that innocent casualties are too often simply counted as strategic factors. The warring parties usually only enter into a ceasefire when they are convinced that they can't win militarily. That is not the case in this situation: Hezbollah clearly believes that they have won this round; and Israel, for its part, remains strongly determined that it will not lose the war.

I was involved in leading a component of the peace negotiations between the government of Sri Lanka and the Tamil Tigers in 2002, and learned a few critical things about ceasefires. A ceasefire needs to be understood fundamentally as a temporary arrangement. If it is to be anything more than an exercise in the art of holding one's breath, it must be turned into an opportunity to help the parties move beyond the perpetual cycle of this win-lose game. Essentially, and somewhat ironically, that means using the period of the ceasefire to help the two sides accept the basic fact that, whether they like it or not, they are in each other's futures, and must face the immediate and practical task of figuring out how to be in some kind of realistic and reasonable relationship with each other.

Unfortunately, there is a powerful temptation on the part of peacekeepers to focus solely on keeping the two sides apart. And since the ceasefire itself results in an enormous improvement in living conditions for most people, there is also a powerful temptation on the part of the general public to see that as good enough. Taken together, these natural tendencies can deepen the separation of the two sides, and cause them to avoid any effort to come to terms with the enemy, or with the issues underlying the conflict. Peace negotiations then tend to become primarily a matter of hammering out compromises limited by untenable preconditions and mutually exclusive ultimate demands. As such, they are generally doomed to failure.

In a situation of deep conflict, a mere separation of military forces is too fragile an arrangement to be sustainable over the longer term. It can be undermined in a moment by an individual act – a political assassination, or a rogue act of terrorism. Furthermore, strategies based on avoidance and compromise tend only to reinforce the "win-lose power struggle," as the basis of the interaction between the two sides, and any resolution, can only be seen as temporary – a holding position until the term of the agreement expires or one side perceives some new advantage or threat, such as better weapons, a stronger leader, and so on.

If a conflict is about anything that really matters – where identity or basic values or survival are at stake – a viable resolution is most likely to be found in a process that enables all parties to create a new basis for their relationship, and to work on creating something fundamentally new together. To be successful in building peace, a ceasefire and subsequent negotiations must be approached not as an invitation to an alternative form of fighting – with words instead with of guns – nor as an effort to turn the suspension of hostilities into a permanent stalemate or standoff.

To build peace, conditions should be created that will allow the conflicting parties to collaborate in a process that will define and develop the terms of their relationship rather than reinforce the terms of their separation. The parties and the international community should be judged on the basis of their willingness to support and engage in such a process of collaborative negotiation. Without such efforts and commitments, we should all simply prepare for the next crisis.

33 Terror

Any experienced military leader will tell you that there are
two basic things you need if you want to undertake a war
with any hope of success: first, a set of objectives that are
clear and realistic; and second, a respectful understanding
of the enemy. Five full years into the War on Terror, it is apparent that little progress has been made in relation to either
of those fundamental requirements.

This should not be too surprising. The way the war has
been conceptualized – as a conflict set within an imagined
world of moral absolutes – seems designed to defy any pragmatic approach that might achieve specific goals or secure
a resolution. One indicator of this failure is that those who
promote and motivate support for the war do so by nurturing a spirit of fear among us, rather than by cultivating a
more positive sense of conviction in the cause. It may be easy
enough to rally public support around a promise of perpetual
safety, but it's impossible to deliver on that promise without
obsessive vigilance. We are left with a stark vision of a world
consumed by war without end.

Perhaps the greatest failure of the war has been the inability of our political leaders to come to grips with the nature of the enemy – terrorists and terrorism. For the most part, they continue to portray the Taliban, al-Qaeda, Hezbollah, and other groups as crazed, ultra-conservative, religious fanatics – what President Bush has begun referring to as "Islamo-fascists." There are, no doubt, some of these elements on both sides, but such caricatures only serve to distract us from the rather unpleasant truth that terrorism is a despicable but rational choice in war. That is, terrorism simply refers to a particular military strategy selected from among others, on the basis of a heartless cost-benefit analysis.

Acts of terrorism are not the specific expression of any religious tradition, and are no more inherently characteristic of one faith than another. Most of the key techniques of terrorism in the modern era – ethnic cleansing, mass abductions and disappearances, suicide bombing, and even flying aircraft into office towers – were pioneered by the Tamil Tigers, a group that is secular and Marxist in ethos. The civil war in Sri Lanka is, in one sense, a struggle between the majority Sinhalese Buddhist and the minority Tamil Hindu communities. But no one familiar with that situation would ever refer to it as a religious conflict, or conclude that the acts of mass terrorism that have marked it reflect Buddhist or Hindu values.

Indeed, the available research suggests that, regardless of the rhetoric surrounding them, individuals who commit acts of terrorism are not likely to be primarily motivated by religious beliefs. The best study, done by Robert Pape of the

University of Chicago, analyzed 38 of the 41 suicide bombings carried out by Hezbollah against American, French,
and Israeli targets during the terror campaign in Lebanon
between 1982 and 1986. Pape found that only eight of the
bombers could be described as "Islamic fundamentalists."
Most – 27 of the bombers – were members of communist or
socialist political organizations, and three were Christians.
Pape concluded:

> What these suicide attackers – and their heirs today
> – shared was not a religious or political ideology but
> simply a commitment to resisting foreign occupa-
> tion... Since suicide terrorism is mainly a response
> to foreign occupation and not Islamic fundamen-
> talism, the use of heavy military force to trans-
> form Muslim societies over there is only likely to
> increase the number of suicide terrorists coming
> at us.[1]

The other key factor that generates terrorism is the experience of injustice without hope of recourse – a condition
epitomized by the brutal and illegal detention system that
continues to hold thousands of individuals at Guantanamo
Bay, Baghram Air Base, and other facilities operated by the
United States throughout the Middle East and elsewhere.

Eliza Grizwold, who accompanied lawyers in Afghanistan sent to interview families of detainees, reported an exchange with a young student whose brother was being held
at Baghram: "He said that a guard had used a cell phone to

take a photograph of his brother's pulverized face, and that if no one would help him he was considering becoming a suicide bomber."[2]

According to the United Nations, the poppy crop that is about to be harvested in Afghanistan will be the largest ever recorded. Satellite images indicate that, despite the official eradication program supported by Canada and the other NATO forces, it will be at least 40 percent larger than last year. The Afghan poppy crop is the main source of heroin in the world, and also the main source of revenue for the Taliban. The crop is an indication that farmers see no economic alternative available to them. It is also a vote of non-confidence in the version of freedom, security, and justice they have been promised.

What people *do* see are the constant war and the prisons and the foreign armies occupying their home lands. Some five years after declaring victory in Iraq, the United States faces ever increasing casualties, and continues to destroy that country at a cost of more than $250 million per day. According to a recent unanimous report involving some 13 security agencies of the U.S. government, the war in Iraq, the front line of the War on Terror, has actually generated an increased threat of terror throughout the world for at least the next generation.

If people feel invisible and trapped, they will inevitably become enraged. If they are consistently ignored and treated as being of no consequence, they will lash out. They may slip to the margins, and the targets of their wrath may at times seem inappropriate, even self-destructive, but they *will* nevertheless lash out. After five years of seeking to punish and suppress all those who would or might be expected to lash out, it is time we changed course in this contemptible disaster we call the War on Terror.

---

1 Robert Pape, *Dying to Win: The Strategic Logic of Suicide Terrorism* (New York: Random House, 2005).
2 Eliza Griswold, "American Gulag: Prisoners' Tales from the War on Terror," *Harper's*, September 2006.

34 Agenda

When the Canadian government, then under Prime Minister Paul Martin, originally undertook to participate in the NATO combat mission in Afghanistan, it was understood to be a defined commitment until February 2007. Under the new government of Prime Minister Stephen Harper, Parliament agreed by a margin of three votes to extend that commitment until "at least 2009."

That was before almost anybody in the country fully understood that this "mission" was to be a war led by NATO, and not a UN peacekeeping operation. Since then, the fact that we are participants in a war has become increasingly clear to everyone as the progress of the mission in Afghanistan has come to be measured solely in the language of body-counts and body-bags. As a result, polls indicate that most Canadians are deeply concerned or actually opposed to the new posture we have asked our military to adopt, and to the reasons behind it.

The prime minister has recently told American audiences that he doesn't believe the polls, or that Canadians are increasingly opposed to the war. Rather, he believes that we are simply distressed by the deaths of Canadian soldiers. I believe that the prime minister is mistaken in this, and that Canadians *are* upset about both the principle and the practical reality of the war. Regardless of how we may understand or judge these issues, what the prime minister has yet to demonstrate is whether he actually cares one way or another about what Canadians think or feel about the war.

Our military depends upon the civilian, political leadership to set clear objectives and defined limits for their operations. The government has now announced that even 2009 is no longer the basis for planning, but has declared to the world that Canada is committed until "peace and security is fully restored in Afghanistan." This worries me, because peace and security has not existed in Afghanistan in living memory, and because the "democratic" government we are supporting there is largely made up of yesterday's warlords in new suits.

Even more worrying is that at least some senior members of the military leadership seem to share this sense of reckless self-delusion. Our civilian leadership depends upon the military to provide clear advice based on cold appraisals of the situation and realistic assessments of what is possible. At the end of Operation Medusa, the first major action of the new mission, the senior commander of the NATO forces had the temerity to declare it an unqualified success, claiming that some 512 Taliban fighters had been killed.

Embarrassingly, he acknowledged that NATO was not able to "verify" the deaths with actual bodies, but he nevertheless boldly asserted that the Taliban had been "completely eradicated" from the region. Millions of Russian veterans, and hundreds of thousands of American soldiers in Iraq, must have been shaking their heads in bewilderment and asking, "Eradicated? After two weeks of combat? Are these people completely ignorant of the Taliban, or of Afghanistan, or of the Middle East, or of Asia?"

Sadly, within a few days, another four Canadians were killed in precisely the same area by a single member of the Taliban with a bomb and a bicycle. A few days later, two more soldiers were dead. The NATO brass simply cleared their throats, declared it a tragedy, and appealed for more troops.

Whatever our opinion of his record may be, the political scholar and former U.S. Secretary of State Henry Kissinger certainly knew a thing or two about the fickleness and the futility of fighting guerrilla wars in Asia. One of his axioms goes something like this: for the insurgency, to not be completely destroyed by the state is victory – for the state, to not completely destroy the insurgents is defeat.

Speaking of the Taliban and considering the controversies over the length of our military commitment – 2007, 2009, whenever, forever – a front-line, middle-ranking Canadian officer in Afghanistan recently made a wise comment that put this truth even more pointedly: "We have all the watches, they have all the time."

In his first speech to the United Nations, Prime Minister Harper made it clear that Afghanistan will be the major

focus of our forces and finances – and the primary preoc-
cupation of our foreign policy – for the foreseeable future.
It will increasingly become the excuse for what we *cannot*
do or achieve as a nation. This is perhaps the real tragedy,
because, while there is certainly work to be done in Afghanistan, there are more pressing and appropriate global priorities, where Canada's contribution is needed and where our
leadership could make a real difference.

My short-list includes the following:

1. Climate change: This is probably the single most sig-
    nificant threat to the well-being of both our own
    country and the planet as a whole. The degradation
    and breakdown of the environment continues inexo-
    rably, accompanied by a spirit of political denial and
    a vacuum of vision in the international community.
    We desperately need leadership that will speak the
    truth and show the way.

2. AIDS: Every day, 1,400 of the world's children die
    and another 1,800 children are newly infected with
    HIV/AIDS. That's almost 1.2 million children who
    will lose their lives or their futures this year as a re-
    sult of a single preventable disease. Just consider the
    long-term devastating impact the illness and deaths
    of these children will have on their communities,
    and on whole nations. Less than 10 percent of the
    children infected, or the orphans left by AIDS vic-
    tims, currently receive care or support. That's just
    counting the children, not the adults. Correcting the

situation is simply a matter of money and commitment. What are we doing with ours?

3. Human security: Peacekeeping forces and diplomatic
    initiatives are urgently required in Darfur, Lebanon,
    and Sri Lanka, to protect millions of civilians and
    to create space for long-term solutions to conflict to
    emerge. Canada has a unique capacity to provide the
    skills, experience, and credibility not only to address
    these situations, but also to spearhead a renewal of
    international peacekeeping.

4. Multilateralism: As a friendly and supportive neigh-
    bour, Canada could help create conditions that would
    enable the United States to move away from the de-
    structive unilateralism that has marked the post-9/11
    period. This would require restoring the relevance
    and effectiveness of the UN system, by making in-
    vestment in and achievement of the Millennium De-
    velopment Goals – which all countries supposedly
    already endorse and could rally around – a priority.

5. Dialogue: Canada could offer a legitimate leadership
    role by promoting cross-cultural understanding and
    reconciliation, thereby creating serious and positive
    alternatives to the global "clash of civilizations."

Now that's an alternative, non-partisan agenda I could get
behind.

35 Intelligence

Finally, some rational voices have begun to speak up from within the military and security establishments of the Western powers. Of course, their message has been quickly silenced or sidelined. But we can still hope that these tiny tentative cracks in the fortress may signal the beginning of a move to honestly face up to the disastrous reality of our military adventures in the Middle East. As Leonard Cohen sings, "There is a crack in everything – that's how the light gets in!"[1]

It began with the release of the annual National Intelligence Estimate, a joint assessment carried out by the CIA and by more than a dozen agencies in the U.S. government responsible for national security. The report confirmed what virtually every scholar in the field has been shouting for the past five years: that the American occupation of Iraq is fueling radicalism and instability in the Islamic world, that the war is the single greatest factor generating global terrorism, and that the "War on Terror" has made the world less safe for all of us.

The authoritative government report concluded that the best contribution America could make to reducing terrorism would be to leave Iraq! As one Congressional leader put it, the report "is nothing less than a declaration by the president's own lieutenants that the emperor has no clothes." The media was soon distracted by another sex scandal, so the report was easily swept aside.

Next came George McGovern, the former U.S. Senator and current UN Global Ambassador on Hunger, who published a solid proposal for withdrawing U.S. forces from Iraq. The exit strategy is designed to reconstruct Iraq, restore some of America's moral credibility, and save the U.S. public accounts from collapse under an unmanageable burden of debt.

The plan would be financed by a small fraction of the money that is currently being squandered by the war. In its determined dedication to destruction in Iraq, the government of our friends to the south invests more than $10 million an hour to fund the war. That amounts to some $250 million a day, every day! World hunger and most communicable diseases could be eradicated for much, much less. The proposal was ignored.

Then, the chief of the General Staff of the British army publicly declared that the presence of British troops in Iraq "exacerbates the security problems," and that they should "get out some time soon." General Sir Richard Dannatt promptly received a severe tongue lashing from his political masters. Nevertheless, British forces have quietly begun to withdraw from parts of Iraq and Afghanistan, perhaps hoping that no one will notice. After all, the point is that our main enemy in Iraq and elsewhere in the Middle East is *us*.

Unfortunately, the same reality applies to Canada. Whether we like or intend it or not, and no matter how hard we try to pretend otherwise, the fact is that in the eyes of most Muslims in the region we are just the agents of yet another Western military occupation of Islamic lands. It matters little whether the occupying forces are Russians, Americans, Brits, Dutch, or Canadians – we inevitably represent the latest expression of the 1000-year war between Islam and the West. Having declared that we intend to stay indefinitely, we have foolishly announced our willingness to serve as targets of the deeply-rooted hostility this terrible tradition inspires.

The bottom line is that any military occupation of a Muslim country by Western forces, regardless of the purpose, is in and of itself intolerable to much of the local population. It is worth remembering that Osama bin Laden's main stated complaint against America is, ostensibly, the presence of U.S. forces at permanent military bases in Saudi Arabia, his homeland, and in other Gulf states. The occupation of Afghanistan by NATO forces allows the Taliban to presume to stand as heroes defending the integrity of the Islamic world, and to command a measure of respect from the Afghan people, regardless of whether they support the other aspects of the Taliban's ideology or not.

Prime Minister Harper has stated that Canadians do not "cut and run." I wonder whatever happened to discretion being the better part of valor and, anyway, who said anything about running? We should definitely honour, like all the other NATO partners, our original commitment. We should make a long-term commitment to providing financial and technical support to Afghanistan. And, most importantly, we should work to convince and support other Muslim nations – such as Morocco, Egypt, Bangladesh, and Indonesia – to provide the necessary peacekeeping forces. They are more likely to be accepted and effective.

[1] Leonard Cohen, "Anthem," *Strange Music: Selected Poems and Songs* (Toronto: McLelland and Steward, 1993).

36 Lists

The UN Secretary General, Kofi Annan, has stepped down after two tumultuous terms in office. His ten years as the world's senior diplomat were marked by some great achievements, as reflected in the awarding of the Nobel Peace Prize to him in 2001 for the renewal of the UN. His term was also marked by some of the worst crises faced by the international community.

I met Mr. Annan only once, at a ceremony in Paris in 1998. He had agreed to accept, on behalf of the international community, a petition containing more than ten million signatures that had been gathered by Amnesty International from people from every country in the world. At the time, there was a concerted effort by a number of countries to dilute international human rights law on the grounds that the standards were simply an expression of Western cultural values.

The petition asserted that, in fact, ordinary people in all societies support and lay claim to a shared vision of human dignity – even if their governments may sometimes find that inconvenient. Kofi Annan's willingness to receive the petition was a demonstration of his own dedication to human rights. Before becoming Secretary General, Annan had headed the UN's peacekeeping operations and, particularly as an African, he had taken the abject failure of the international community to prevent the genocide in Rwanda as a personal responsibility. His first initiative in reforming the UN was to make the promotion and protection of human rights an operational priority for every agency within the international system.

In my view, Kofi Annan leaves an important legacy and challenge that is captured in two simple lists. The first is the list of Millennium Development Goals, the eight critically urgent needs that all governments recognized and signed on to in September 2000 as global priorities to be achieved by 2015. They are:

- to cut extreme poverty and hunger by half,
- to reduce child mortality by two-thirds,
- to reduce maternal mortality by two-thirds,
- to make elementary level education available to all children,
- to eliminate gender disparity in post-elementary education,
- to halt and begin to reverse the spread of AIDS and malaria,
- to ensure environmental sustainability,
- to develop a global partnership for development.

The MDGs remain the stated priorities of the international community, though in almost all cases we are today – halfway to 2015 – even further from achieving them. It is a tragedy and a scandal that governments around the world have again failed to back up their fine declarations with the real money and the political will that is required. Though they are ambitious, fully funding the MDGs would actually cost only a fraction of the money currently being squandered on the war in Iraq.

The second list was also created and agreed to in 2000. Though not as clearly defined by measurable material outcomes, the Manifesto for a Culture of Peace recognized that each of us has a real and direct part to play in securing the future of humanity. It appealed to all persons and communities to pledge themselves to fostering six key values:

- respect all life: to respect the life and dignity of each human being without discrimination or prejudice;
- reject violence: to practice active non-violence, rejecting violence in all its forms: physical, sexual, psychological, economical, and social;
- share with others: to share my time and material resources in a spirit of generosity to put an end to exclusion, injustice, and oppression;
- listen to understand: to defend freedom of expression and cultural diversity, giving preference always to dialogue;
- preserve the planet: to promote consumer behaviour that is responsible and development practices that preserve the balance of nature on the planet;

☞ rediscover solidarity: to contribute to the development of my community, with the full participation of women and respect for democratic principles.

Sadly – no, tragically – the momentum for developing this list as a practical agenda for building a global "Culture of Peace" was quickly displaced, and virtually forgotten, within less than a year by the declaration of the "War on Terror." The ethic based on these six key values was summarily supplanted by a single and very different, but also very explicitly stated value that remains dominant today: "Those who are not with us are against us."

I hope these two lists will not be lost in the transition from one Secretary General to another. After all, the needs they reflect have only grown deeper as each year passes, and the solutions they represent are ever more essential to the survival of our planet, of our species, and of our communities – indeed, to the survival of individual human dignity.

37 Accountability

As the endgame of the U.S. occupation of Iraq begins to unfold, the question of accountability will increasingly come to
the fore. As has been characteristic of almost every aspect
of this war, an unseemly spectacle of deception and double
standards will increasingly be played out in Baghdad and
in Washington as the issue of "crimes against humanity" is
addressed.

On the one hand, Saddam Hussain was convicted of mass
murder in the case of the 1982 revenge killings of 148 men
and boys in the village of Dujail, and sentenced to hang.
Saddam stated that he preferred to be shot by a firing squad.
While the formalities of an appeal of the death sentence and
a second trial for genocide for the 1987 chemical attacks
on Kurdish villages were commenced, Saddam was quickly
taken from his cell and hanged.

All credible international observers and legal experts denounced the trials as grossly unfair. A detailed examination
by Human Rights Watch concluded that the court reflected "a

basic lack of understanding of fundamental fair trial principles." No one doubted that Saddam was responsible for a long
litany of horrific atrocities committed during the decades he
was in power, and that he had to be held accountable. However, regardless of how heinous his crimes, if the goal of the
whole exercise was the establishment of a society based on
democracy and the rule of law, and the strengthening of the
image of the occupation as fair and legitimate, then the trial
and execution represent yet another abject failure.

The fact is that the trials of Saddam and his henchmen
are being held in Iraq only because the U.S. continues to
oppose the International Criminal Court. The ICC was established by the UN precisely to put an end to impunity for
dictators such as Saddam. In this, it represents one of the real
human rights achievements of the international community
during the past decade. It provides an authoritative and independent means for prosecuting deposed leaders, allowing
the countries they have devastated to focus their efforts on
rebuilding their own legal institutions and social stability.

The U.S. has refused to cooperate with the ICC for two
reasons: first, because the ICC does not allow for the use of
the death penalty; and second, because the U.S. government
will not tolerate the possibility that American soldiers or officials might be subject to prosecution for war crimes under
international law. (Similarly, the U.S. stands as one of only
two countries – the other being Somalia – that refuse to
ratify the Convention on the Rights of the Child, essentially
because that treaty prohibits the execution of people younger
than 18 years of age!)

Hence, instead of handing him over to the UN and advancing the cause of justice, Saddam was subjected to an incompetent political show trial in Baghdad. As has become evident, the civil war raging with ever increasing ferocity in Iraq has nothing to do with any residual loyalty to Saddam. However, the execution of this Sunni former leader at the hands of the new Shia-dominated government after a patently unfair trial has inevitably only deepened the cataclysm.

On the other hand, in Washington, George W. Bush presides over a war that is increasingly recognized as an absurd and illegal fiasco. The main justifications for the invasion – alleged weapons of mass destruction and supposed links between Saddam and al-Qaeda – have been shown to be utterly without foundation at best, and more likely to be complete fabrications. It is telling that Kofi Annan stated on his retirement that his greatest regret after ten years as UN Secretary General was his failure to persuade the U.S. not to invade Iraq.

A great embarrassed silence now covers the question of the cause of the war, as when someone tells a bad joke at a polite dinner party. A deep uncomfortable silence extends to topics such as Abu Ghraib and Guantanamo Bay, as when an awkward family secret is revealed at a reception after a funeral. The purpose of the war now seems to be simply to help establish public security and basic social services in the midst of the chaos and destruction caused by, well, the war.

The U.S. war in Iraq has now gone on longer than the American involvement in World War II. It has claimed far more American lives than were lost in the terrorist attacks of 9/11, and has cost at least $400 billion. It has also resulted in the verified deaths of some 55,000 Iraqi civilians. So far.

The main outcomes of the war have been the destruction of Iraq, the unleashing of a civil war and, according to the recent report of the study group led by former Secretary of State James Baker, the prospect of "escalating costs...greater suffering...growing terrorism... a humanitarian catastrophe... and the sparking of a broader regional war." The report further states starkly that, "The ability of the U.S. to shape outcomes is diminishing. Time is running out." And that increasingly seems like an optimistic view.

It makes one wonder where we should focus our attention when considering the question of "war crimes" and "crimes against humanity." Despite the silence, and beyond the trials and execution of Saddam, the real question of accountability looms.

38 Star

Advent and Christmas are the seasons for celebrating the great promises – peace on earth, the restoration of light, the hope of a new year. For me, the season begins on December 10, when we commemorate the proclamation of the Universal Declaration of Human Rights in 1948. Coming in the aftermath of the Holocaust and the horrors of World War II, the UDHR promised *nunca más*, never again, and declared a global commitment to preventing war and to overcoming oppression.

Of course, for far too many people around the world, these have proven to be false promises. The commitment to action has too often been forgotten or ignored. It is simply scandalous to say the words *nunca más*, never again, in the face of Rwanda, Sierra Leone, Bosnia, East Timor, Sri Lanka, Iraq, Darfur... The list of betrayal seems endless.

The struggle for human rights is not found only in the mass suffering caused by distant wars in Africa and Asia; it is also the stuff of our own communities and daily lives.

It confronts us in the growing gap between rich and poor, and in the ways that gap is increasingly expressed in hunger and in homelessness. It confronts us when our leaders, in the spirit of fear and in the name of security, attempt to persuade us that some people are not entitled to fundamental rights, that is, to be regarded as human. It confronts us in the spreading degradation and destruction of the ecosystem.

In a world with so many intractable troubles and complex challenges, is it really possible to hold any real hope in "new beginnings" – to have faith in the promises of *nunca más*, or in the coming of the light in the midst of such darkness? I continue to cling to that hope, because of an experience I had some years ago in Cambodia, and because of a peasant farmer I met there named Dara, which means "star" in the Khmer language.

The first time I visited Cambodia was after the country had been devastated by decades of horror – the years of secret bombing by the United States, the terror of the mass murders by the Khmer Rouge, and finally the invasion and occupation by the Vietnamese army. Like unexploded bombs buried just below the surface of a rice field or like left-over mines hidden along a forest path, each of these traumas continued to have a devastating impact on the society.

Peace negotiations had finally resulted in an agreement among the warring factions to create a new way forward, and in a commitment by the international community to support them in re-building the country. I was there to work with the emerging government to reform the police and legal systems to be more respectful of human rights.

In some ways it felt as if we were starting from the very beginning. The old government, the Khmer Rouge, had destroyed almost everything. They had tried to kill everyone who could read, or who wore glasses. One of my first meetings was to be with the members of the Supreme Court, except that no one could tell me where to find them. I spent a whole day searching through the city and I finally found one very elderly man sitting beside a single filing cabinet under a shady tree in someone's back garden. *He* was the Supreme Court.

In other ways, it felt as if we were confronting a legacy of violence and of abuse that had gone on forever. On another day I was scheduled to meet with the Minister of National Security, but my transportation had disappeared. No one in the crowd of taxi drivers and street guides who gathered to help me at the main intersection of downtown Phnom Penh knew who the minister was, or where I could find him. Finally I said, "Take me to the headquarters of the bad police." Everyone automatically knew exactly where to go. In a few minutes, an impressive convoy of taxis and *cyclopouces* pulled up in front of a massive wall bearing large stainless steel lettering: "Department of National Security."

Behind the wall, after my meeting, I encountered a man who had been arrested in one of the outlying villages for some small infraction. His name was Dara. A poor peasant farmer, he had clearly been severely beaten. I began to interview him but after a few exchanges he looked confused and asked me, "Sir, why are you asking me these questions? Is something wrong?"

It was my turn to feel confused. Through the interpreter, I said, "Well, Dara, it appears to me that you have been beaten by the police." At that point, the man realized he was speaking to a fool. He spoke with great patience, as if explaining how to add two plus two: "Yes, of course, they are the police and I am a peasant. They caught me and so I was beaten. Naturally, it is the way of things."

Our discussion continued for some time. In one of the truly privileged moments of my life, I witnessed the moment when Dara realized that the "human rights" I was fussing about were supposed to include everyone, *even him*. And in that moment something new happened, something fundamental changed.

My colleagues and I protested Dara's treatment and managed to get him released. As I watched him return home to his family, I knew I was witnessing more than one person's freedom. It was, perhaps, the birth of a whole new future. Once we embrace our humanity and claim our inherent dignity, there is no going back. Bad things will continue to happen and people will still face oppression, but they will know that it is not deserved, and that is not their fate. And even more, they will realize that it is wrong and, with a bit of help and a lot of work, that it can be changed.

The next time I visited Cambodia I went to Dara's village. In what had been a depressed and devastated place, I found a new children's art centre nurturing self-expression, and an active Citizen's Police Consultation Committee promoting public safety instead of national security – chaired by a man named Dara.

Of course, such initiatives are fragile. But even the most tentative of twinkling stars shine across vast distances of cold darkness, and have the power to inspire us. Whenever I feel a sense of despair at the plight of our planet, or at the ways we seem to need to continually relearn the same lessons at such great cost to ourselves and to others, I think of the gleam in Dara's eyes when he became aware that he mattered, and that could he make a difference, and when he did something about it. May this coming year be such a time for all of us.

Photo Credits

Derek Evans has served two terms as Deputy Secretary General of Amnesty International, and has led more than 70 international delegations conducting human rights investigations or peace negotiations. He was formerly Executive Director of the Naramata Centre, one of Canada's foremost experiential learning institutes.

Evans ⟨...⟩ and is the author or co⟨...⟩ous titles published by ⟨...⟩ *The Light and the Burni*⟨...⟩ 2004). More of his work ⟨...⟩ans.com⟩. He is married ⟨...⟩y are parents of three ad⟨...⟩nagan Valley of British ⟨...⟩